Taming the Potte

Taming
the
Potted
Beast

The Strange and Sensational History
of the Not-So-Humble Houseplant

Molly Williams

Illustrated by Ellie Hajdu

Andrews McMeel
PUBLISHING®

Taming the Potted Beast

Andrews McMeel Publishing
a division of Andrews McMeel Universal
1130 Walnut Street, Kansas City, Missouri 64106

www.andrewsmcmeel.com

22 23 24 25 26 RR4 10 9 8 7 6 5 4 3 2 1

ISBN: 978-1-5248-6900-7

Library of Congress Control Number: 2022935718

Editor: Allison Adler
Art Director: Holly Swayne
Production Editor: Thea Voutiritsas and Brianna Westervelt
Production Manager: Julie Skalla

ATTENTION: SCHOOLS AND BUSINESSES

Andrews McMeel books are available at quantity discounts with bulk purchase for educational, business, or sales promotional use. For information, please e-mail the Andrews McMeel Publishing Special Sales Department: specialsales@amuniversal.com.

For Dorothy and her healthy dose of skepticism—
and eternal love and support

Contents

Introduction

The idea for the book you're holding in your hands came to me during a bout of pandemic boredom in 2020. A houseplant lover and constant social media lurker, I was perusing a popular buy-sell-trade Facebook page dedicated to rare houseplants when I randomly stopped on a listing of a philodendron "Pink Princess," a plant I used to see retail back in 2018 for $40. The plant in the online listing was juvenile, had three maturing leaves, and was planted in a four-inch grower's pot.

The January 2020 asking price? Five hundred dollars.

I was blown away.

The price was utterly ridiculous, and it made me wonder how much these folks willing to drop hundreds to thousands of dollars for their dream plants know about the plants that they're spending fortunes on. Did that woman from Chicago in desperate need of a variegated *Alocasia macrorrhiza* "Stingray" know that the object of her desire originated from Southeast Asia? How much do any of us know about this hobby we're all wrapped up in?

So began my adventure into the depths of houseplant history.

So, you might be asking, who is this book for? Is it for plant-o-philes? People obsessed with both horticulture and history? New plant parents? Old plant parents?

Guess what? There's something in this book for everyone! From historical content to DIY plant projects, I've got you covered. The only requirement is that you, the reader, must love houseplants. Or, like most of us, love-hate them.

If you haven't noticed, houseplants are having a major moment, but excitement over plants isn't new. This gargantuan trend has been thousands of years in the making. Houseplants go way, way, way back in history, with colorful and storied timelines of their own, full of historical highs, devastating lows, and sensational turning points along the way.

And here you were thinking that your houseplants were just a nice way to bring nature into your home.

This book will fill in the gaps and unearth the little-known, peculiar history of the houseplant in all its green glory. We'll begin when King Nebuchadnezzar II ordered the Hanging Gardens of Babylon to be built for his new bride, Amytis, and unknowingly set the roots for modern-day houseplant fandom. Then we'll carry on through the ages, learning about the plants that kept company with kings and queens—and, on occasion, threatened to kill them.

After we page through history, we come to the present, where we're overpaying for popular plants and maybe unwittingly contributing to a new botanical black market. Today's plants can be sourced from just about anywhere in the world and from all kinds of purveyors, from outlets as mundane as Walmart to specialty online collectors and fancy-schmancy boutique shops. Fantastic, right? Unfortunately, there's a dark side to this plant fever: it's led to a worldwide plant-poaching problem. Even worse than swiping plants from their natural habitat, garden-variety criminals are driving up the prices of certain "rare" plants, stealing from conservatories and private collections and reselling their loot for big bucks.

The indoor cultivation and domestication of botanical specimens has been a happy hobby for millennia, by all kinds of civilizations and in all kinds of living spaces. From the marble and terra-cotta pots of the Romans to the Victorian terrariums and the miniature plants of multiple Asian cultures, there are secret histories to be told. These are the historic events that have led to the adorable succulents in our office windows and feisty ficuses in our greenhouses. We should be familiar with them.

The pages of this book will take you on an exhilarating botanical adventure through the ages, and each stop will enlighten you with historical context—as well as provide instructions for at-home plant projects. Each chapter includes a section that will help you create and care for an era-appropriate historical houseplant menagerie. You'll learn how to create indoor gardens, grow veggies like ginger and microgreens, tend to your own indoor lemon trees, sculpt a shrub, learn how to nurture a swooning plant back to life, and much more.

Then, after their scandalous history has been revealed and the DIY projects are all done, in the back of the book is a quick and handy reference section called "Timeless Tips for Keeping Your Historical Houseplants Happy." You'll find a handy breakdown of basic houseplant care by plant type. You'll also learn water and light requirements, propagation techniques, buying tips, container selection, and how to quickly identify common pests.

This isn't a comprehensive botanical or historical text. It would be impossible to include every culture and every tributary timeline across the thousands of years that humans have been bringing plants indoors. Think of this book instead as a resource to guide and inform you on your houseplant-collecting journey. I learned *so* much in the process of writing this book, and I can only hope you'll learn just as much in your own exploration of this curious and compelling history.

* Unless noted, all plants mentioned in this book should be considered toxic to pets and are not for human consumption.

Taming
the
Potted
Beast

CHAPTER 1

Leafy Wonders
of the Ancient World

THE NEOLITHIC ERA (10,000–3,000 BCE)

T he journey begins in 10,000 BCE with the first documented evidence of the domestication of plants as crops. This is also known as "how this whole domestic plant fad got started." Are these technically "houseplants"? Nope. Are they important in terms of our story? Absolutely.

This is the beginning of wheat, barley, chickpeas, lentils, and so many other grains that we grow and use today. Get ready to learn about the plants of ancient Mesopotamia and the Fertile Crescent. Then, take a side trip to the Hanging Gardens of Babylon, which are known as one of the seven wonders of the ancient world.

In "Your Leafy Legacy," learn how to create your own Babylon with the most magnificent hanging houseplants. After all is said and done, your home might become one of the wonders of the modern world!

The Agricultural Revolution

What is now called the "agricultural revolution" was when early humans transitioned from nomadic tribes that hunted and gathered into the first civilizations. This transition coincided with the invention of the wheel, the discovery of fire, and the use of hand tools. These developments bridged the gap between the New Stone Age and the Neolithic era and propelled humankind forward.

Around 10,000 BCE, small agricultural settlements began popping up around the Fertile Crescent. The Fertile Crescent, for those of you who don't remember middle school social studies, is the slice of the Middle East that encompasses parts of modern-day Iraq, Syria, Lebanon, Palestine, Israel, Jordan, and Egypt. In the Fertile Crescent, wild barley and wheat had begun to grow as the result of a period of global warming. At the same time, ancient civilizations like Babylonia, Assyria, and Egypt came to power.

These civilizations all developed because of plant domestication. Domestication, meaning when early farmers selected the crops that were easiest to grow and harvest, was essential to a successful early civilization. Basic grains that are still staples today are the same cereals that were cultivated during the Neolithic era. Wheats and barleys were the first crops to be domesticated by the communities that settled down. Then, over time, the same people began domesticating lentils, flax, and chickpeas.

In the Fertile Crescent, crops thrived because of access to the Tigris and Euphrates Rivers. Geographically—and historically—plants, people, and animals all benefit from having access to the fertile lands that surround powerful rivers. In this case, the water from both the Tigris and the Euphrates provided irrigation for civilization's first farms. This was the beginning of Mesopotamia, Greek for "land between rivers."

Those ancient farms succeeded, and the communities around them began to grow. At the same time, developing societies in Asia and the Americas started on a similar path. Maize and rice were cultivated and farmed, to enormous success.

Without those first initial roots (pun intended) and the domestication of crops, we wouldn't be caring for houseplants of our own today.

Ancient Mesopotamian Gardens

The social centers of Babylonia and Assyria consisted of temples and courtyards where people would gather daily. These spaces were loaded with plants—in particular, trees. So much so that these spaces were basically miniature arboretums.

Ancient cities were built within the confines of tall walls that kept the bad guys, wild animals, and flood waters out of the city. Within those walls lived bustling, successful metropolises. Because of the wild, unpredictable nature of life outside the walls, gardens were predominantly urban features.

The people who lived in these cities planted gardens everywhere they could. City and palace courtyards, around temples, and the roofs of buildings were all fair game.

Almost always, these gardens had a central feature: a tree.

These trees were mostly species that produce delicious-smelling blooms and incredible fruits. With those trees, the people created their concept of paradise. The tree frequently represented a god—particularly in Islamic gardens.

It wasn't uncommon, especially in the massive courtyards of royal palaces, to find exotic animals and plants of all kinds—some being the spoils of battle and some being generous gifts from neighboring kingdoms.

Some kingdoms had cities so large that they were able to house orchards inside the city walls. Advancements in irrigation and aqueducts meant that fresh water was readily available to keep the fruit orchards producing.

The gardens were a life source for Mesopotamia. These public spaces were where people would go to gather and to collect and harvest food to sustain their families. Gardens made these walled cities home.

The Mythical Hanging Gardens of Babylon

Tending to a houseplant can be delightfully sensual, romantic even. It takes routine love and a soft touch to coax these plants into showing off for us outside of their natural habitats. After all, houseplants aren't native to the indoors, and they didn't grow legs and walk into our living rooms. Bringing these green jewels into your home for indoor cultivation is a bit of a trick.

One of the earliest, possibly mythical examples of the romantic power of plants was found in ancient Mesopotamia, where the ingenious inhabitants developed newfangled concepts like the wheel, mathematics, astronomy, and writing in cursive. Let's go all the way back to 605 BCE to the city of Babylon, located in modern-day Iraq. This also happens to be the location of the earliest records of plant ownership outside of cultivating crops. The city itself was roughly the size of Chicago and housed the famed Hanging Gardens of Babylon—which are now known as one of the seven wonders of the ancient world, and one of the greatest disputed landmarks of all time.

Academics, historians, and archaeologists have spent thousands of years debating the existence of these gardens. Both ancient Greek and Roman texts paint elaborate pictures of lush, green plants draping and cascading along the 75-foot-high terrace walls of the city of Babylon. The walls were so thick that Babylonians routinely held chariot races along the top of them. Plants and flowers of all kinds decorated the palace, creating an oasis of flora in the middle of the desert.

The gardens were built in a semicircular layout and were tiered on man-made hills that reached the tops of the city walls. Trees and flora also grew on top of the city's roofs, creating a garden that spanned the length of a football field. A gargantuan feat for its time, it had to be irrigated with a minimum of 30,000 liters of water from a tributary of the Euphrates that ran through the middle of Babylon.

Maybe these gardens existed, but maybe they didn't.

The story is titillating. It goes like this: In the year 605 BCE, King Nebuchadnezzar married Amytis, a princess from Media (in modern-day Iran). Even though the palace of King Nebuchadnezzar was grand, Amytis longed for the lush greenery of her homeland. Wanting to please his new bride, the king built the famed Hanging Gardens of Babylon to ease her homesickness. The Greek historian Diodorus Siculus described the garden as ". . . sloped like a hillside and the several parts of the structure rose from one another tier on tier. On all this, the earth had been piled and was thickly planted with trees of every kind that, by their great size and other charm, gave pleasure to the beholder. The water machines raised the water in great abundance from the river in a way that no one could see it."

Because of Siculus's description, it has been widely debated as to whether or not the gardens were actually hanging from the roofs and ceilings of buildings or if they were planted along the tops of terraces and the plants were trained to drape downward. Either way, it would have taken great feats in architecture and design strategy to make it work. The plants would have needed irrigation, which seems almost impossible in the middle of the desert. And, of course, this is all speculation because no physical evidence of the gardens has ever been found, despite the continual efforts by archaeologists. Where did all this confusion and speculation come from, exactly?

After they had captured the city of Babylon in 331 BCE, the Greek army went galivanting home with all kinds of exaggerated stories of the famed city. They told tales of monstrous gardens, humongous buildings, and riches they could have never imagined. These boys and men didn't have a clue about the likes of Nebuchadnezzar's famous palace (even though Nebuchadnezzar himself was long gone by that time) or the great Temple of Belus. As these stories were passed around ancient Greece, the tales grew and grew until Babylon became infamous.

Intertwined in these stories were elaborate descriptions of plants. There were massive palm trees and flora as far as the eye could see. Plants were growing on the roofs, the walls, and hanging from the ceilings of buildings. Even though the city of Babylon was surrounded by desert, it was brimming with green, lush life. To these storytelling outsiders, the city must have seemed like a mirage.

Archaeologists have unearthed tablets from the time of Nebuchadnezzar's kingdom, but there are no mentions of these fantastical gardens. Recently an irrigation well was discovered near where the palace is thought to have stood. However, there is much chatter in the archaeological community about whether the location is actually the correct one. Strabo, the ancient Greek geographer and historian, placed Nebuchadnezzar's palace in a very specific location away from the Euphrates River. It is now widely believed that the location is completely inaccurate and that those initial stories told by soldiers may have been about another Mesopotamian city altogether.

That famous debate rattles the entire myth. What if the famous Hanging Gardens of Babylon weren't located in Babylon at all?

In 2013 Oxford-based historian Dr. Stephanie Dalley came forward, claiming she had finally pieced together the mystery of the gardens' actual locations. Dr. Dalley posited that the gardens were built in Nineveh by Assyrian ruler Sennacherib, not King Nebuchadnezzar of Babylon.

This hypothesis didn't come to Dalley out of nowhere. Dr. Dalley first proposed the idea to her peers back in 1991, but it took her over two decades to pull together the evidence to prove her theory. It all started with a piece of historical information (as most research detective work does). An artifact from Sennacherib's palace vividly and explicitly shows trees growing on top of a colonnade, just like the second-hand accounts of the famed gardens claimed.

From there, Dr. Dalley searched for other historical evidence. She compared Babylonian and Assyrian topography, scoured ancient texts, and came out certain that the gardens were built in Nineveh, not Babylon. Her book *The Mystery of the Hanging Garden of Babylon* was published in 2013 and documented her compiled evidence.

There are as many naysayers and skeptics as those who believe Dr. Dalley's theory. Regardless, the story of the Hanging Gardens of Babylon is as enchanting as ever, whether myth or historical reality.

YOUR LEAFY LEGACY:
Six Hanging Houseplants for Your Own Palace Garden

Who wouldn't want to live in a home adorned with hundreds of hanging plants? Well, hundreds might be overkill—not everyone has the amount of disposable time it would take to care for all those green babies. No matter, the following plants are easy to hang and (sometimes) easy to love. You'll have your own Babylon before you know it.

* Unless noted, all these queens can grow in traditional potting mix. If you're potting them in a container with no drainage, be careful not to overwater.

Satin Pothos

Scindapsus pictus

This plant is the epitome of luxury. If you've been searching for a textured leaf that also gives you hanging-garden vibes, look no further. The Satin Pothos can drape from a smaller container, or it can be trained to climb up a totem, giving you the height of a tree and the look of a vine. The silky leaf texture lends to the glimmer these give off in the sun. They're resilient plants, so if you miss a watering cycle, don't worry—this plant will forgive you.

> **Light:** *Indirect*
> **Water:** *Weekly, or when the soil is dry to the touch*
> **Native Habitat:** *India, Bangladesh, Thailand, Malaysia, Borneo, Java, Sumatra, and the Philippines*

Giant Tillandsia

Tillandsia xerographica

These big guys are the stars of the tillandsia family. Otherwise known as air plants, tillandsia have been known as "easy" houseplants simply because they don't require soil to survive. While they're not exactly easy as the marketing may have led you to believe, they are easy to design with. Because they don't need soil to survive, you can plop these plants anywhere. You can hang them from the ceiling or place them on shelves and windowsills. This plant's larger size allows them to drape or hang without much effort on your part. You can get creative and hang a bunch of them from the ceiling like mobiles! The only thing better than a hanging plant is one that rotates, mesmerizing its housemates.

> **Light:** *Bright, indirect. If you think about their natural environment, they're found dangling in the canopy of the rain forest. Try to re-create that.*
> **Water:** *Mist two times per week or soak them in a bowl of distilled water once per week. Let the plant dry before putting it back.*
> **Native Habitat:** *Southern Mexico, El Salvador, Guatemala, and Honduras*

String of Hearts

Ceropegia woodii

A mature String of Hearts plant is glamorous enough to give Queen Amytis a run for her money. The plant itself is delicate looking, but when given the right amount of water and light, it is very hardy. When a String of Hearts plant has enough space to hang, she'll grow up to twelve feet long! Once your plant starts growing, you'll notice that it will quickly tangle into itself and become a maze of vines. It helps to gently adjust the plant weekly to keep it from turning into a mess. You don't want to be sitting on the floor a few months later trying to untangle a multifoot-long plant. It's a real pain.

Light: *Bright, indirect. Even though it's semisucculent, it doesn't like direct sun.*
Water: *Weekly, when the soil is dry to the touch. Do not overwater.*
Native Habitat: *South Africa*

Window-Leaf Monstera

Monstera obliqua

The *Monstera obliqua* is an elusive plant. A lot of folks accidentally buy a *Monstera adansonii* (a pretty cool plant in its own right) thinking that they've found a true *M. obliqua*. A lot of plants are misadvertised as well. It is said that there have only been a handful of instances where the *M. obliqua* has been sighted in the wild, making it very difficult to believe that some online sellers can ethically deliver what they're promising. There probably isn't a true *M. obliqua* out there in cultivation, and what is being sold as one is simply a hybrid. Probably. There is a lot of speculation on the subject. The closest thing to real that I've found is through the extremely reputable NSE Tropicals in south Florida, where a single four-inch plant recently sold for $2,900.

The main difference between an *M. adansonii* and an *M. obliqua* is the size of the holes, called fenestrations, in the leaves. The *M. obliqua* looks like there's barely any leaf hanging on in between the massive holes. The *M. adansonii* has significantly more leaf mass. That said, some leaves on the *M. obliqua* don't have holes at all!

While other monsteras have the reputation of being "easy" to grow, *M. obliqua* is a true exception to the rule. They are notoriously difficult to grow and require a continuously humid environment and damp soil to thrive. If you manage to get one, place it somewhere that gets bright, indirect light and then fret over it day and night.

The bottom line is if you fall in love with the look of the *M. obliqua* but don't have a couple thousand bucks to spend on one, go get a lovely *M. adansonii* instead.

Light: *Bright, indirect*

Water: *Two times per week, and monitor closely. Don't let the soil dry out.*

Native Habitat: *Peru and various other locations in Central and South America*

Rock Tassel Fern

Lycopodium squarrosum

This plant might be the best one to snatch up if you're trying to create your own Gardens of Babylon vibe. The Rock Tassel Fern is a true prehistoric plant. These ancient, tree-sized plants used to be one of the dominant forms of plant life on this planet. While it carries the "fern" name, it's actually part of the club moss family, *Lycopodiaceae*. The plant has long, draping tassels that can grow up to nine feet long in prime conditions. Rock Tassel Ferns prefer indirect light and moist soil. They need a loose, epiphytic planting mix rich in bark and peat.

Rock Tassel Ferns can sometimes be difficult to find on the buyer's market, so if you find one it would behoove you to scoop it up!

Light: *Indirect light*

Water: *Two times per week minimum. Don't let the soil dry out.*

Native Habitat: *Africa, Polynesia, Australia, and Asia—particularly in the eastern Himalayas and Malaysia.*

Shingle Plant

Rhaphidophora cryptantha

Take it upon yourself to wander around a local botanic garden, and you'll probably find one of these beauties growing up the wall. Not only does the stem cling to the vertical surface that it's climbing, the leaves do too. This creates a very interesting, eye-catching growth pattern that was made for the Gardens of Babylon!

Shingle Plants love warmer temperatures, so don't let your indoor temps drop below 60 degrees Fahrenheit. This plant also grows best in bright, indirect light with moderate watering. Don't let the soil dry out all the way, but also don't drown your plant. Give the soil a feel before watering.

Light: *Bright, indirect*
Water: *Weekly, when soil starts to dry to the touch*
Native Habitat: *Papua New Guinea*

CHAPTER 2

That Time Cleopatra Tried to Poison Mark Antony

ANCIENT EGYPTIANS, ROMANS, AND GREEKS (3,000 BCE–350 CE)

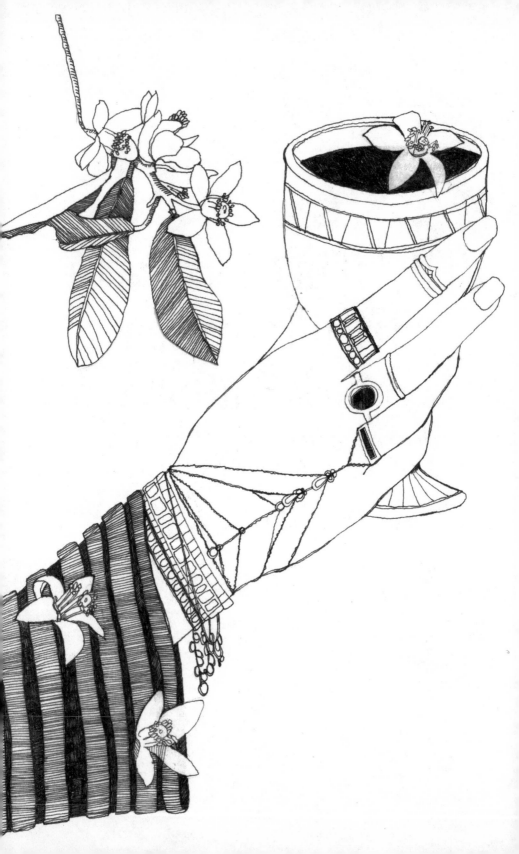

T he ancient Egyptians, Romans, and Greeks all kept cultivated plants for decoration. There were plants everywhere in the homes and public spaces of these ancient powers—from courtyards to temples, even on barges. Over a few thousand years, plants went from being utilitarian to serving as status symbols. Greek botanist Theophrastus wrote *Historia Plantarum* between 350 BCE and 287 BCE, the very first gardening guide! In it, he attempted to classify plants based on their reproduction methods—a first in the history of botany.

Ancient Egypt

Ancient Egypt. That name conjures images of grand pyramids rising from the desert and royalty draped in rich, jewel-toned cloth. The ancient Egyptian civilization spanned thousands of years, roughly from 3100 to 30 BCE. We are as close in historical time to Cleopatra as Cleopatra was to the building of the Great Pyramids. From the Naqada III, the last phase of Egyptian prehistory, to the Ptolemaic period, an entire history exists—far too much to cover here. But one thing we can explore, and can learn from, is how ancient Egyptians loved their plants.

Every aspect of life in ancient Egypt relied on the Nile River. The Nile was their life source. The first ancient Egyptian gardens belonged to wealthy residences and temples that could afford to channel water from the Nile to keep their plants happy. Many of these gardens were utilitarian at first and used to grow vegetables and other edible plants for use in religious ceremonies.

It wasn't until the New Kingdom, around 1520 BCE, that Egyptians started planting ornamental gardens. Later referred to as pleasure gardens, these plots became common in all wealthy, luxurious abodes. There were water features with fish, grapevines, lotus blossoms, and trees. There were also flower beds full of roses, poppies, jasmine, anemones, daisies, and mums. We can assume that these gardens were absolutely gorgeous.

Plants at this time signaled wealth and status. During his reign, Pharaoh Thutmose III brought more than 300 plants from Syria back to Egypt. Around the same time, it was recorded that trade began between Egypt and other surrounding powers, and plants and flowers were one of the main products traded. Even Queen Hatshepsut grew frankincense in her personal temple.

Living space for ancient Egyptians was an indoor/outdoor situation. Homes, estates, and palaces had open-air courtyards that connected directly to the indoor living spaces. Even the poorest of the poor people had outdoor living space in the form of balconies and rooftops.

And plants were everywhere.

In fact, the ancient Egyptians were the first civilization to use containers for outdoor plants. Gardeners used containers to make their plants mobile so they could be moved around to the prime growing environment. Over the years they utilized this concept with plants for indoor/outdoor decoration.

Plants were constantly moved in, out, and around the living spaces of ancient Egypt. They were placed on royal barges and in public spaces. They decorated sacred temples. The plants of ancient Egypt became more than just utilitarian; they were decorative as well—and brought the people who cared for them great joy.

The name "Cleopatra" is synonymous with ancient Egypt, even though her reign during the Ptolemaic period clocked in right at the end of what we refer to as "ancient" times. She's a pop-culture icon (looking at you, Elizabeth Taylor), the topic of many bestselling biographies, and, unfortunately, more than a few misinformed Halloween costumes.

Cleopatra is popular, even 2,051 years after her death. She is both a myth and a legend as tales of her fiery, obsessive personality have traveled through time. While there are many things we do not know, and will never know, about Cleopatra, one thing we do know is that she was enthralled with poison and the effects it had on people. Allegedly, her way out of the world of the living was through a self-served deadly bite from an asp.

During her life, she experimented hundreds of times with poisons. As in, she tested them on living things. Cleopatra was interested in the correct dosage for different levels of toxicity. She was especially intrigued with fatal doses. She played around with various combinations of poisons, most derived directly from her gardens, and she performed many of these experiments in front of an audience, usually at dinner parties, where her husband, Mark Antony, was present.

Cleopatra and Antony's relationship was childish, passionate, and full of distrust for each other. So, it's no surprise that Antony would fear meeting his end at the hand of his wife. The story goes that he would refuse to eat or drink anything unless Cleopatra had tasted it first.

Eventually, Cleopatra found a loophole. She coated nontoxic, ornamental flowers with a poison, something concocted with poison hemlock, and had a servant adorn Antony's dinner clothes with them. She then had the servant weave unpoisoned flowers of the same kind into her own clothes. At the party, she plucked a bloom from her own dress and placed it in her wine chalice, and told Antony to do the same, so their wine would taste like the flowers. He agreed and followed suit. Just as he was about to drink the wine, Cleopatra laughed in his face and told him what she had done, reportedly saying something like, "If it were possible for me to live without you, how easy it would be for me to devise ways and means to kill you." Antony called what he thought was her bluff, so Cleopatra forced a servant to drink his wine. The poor servant promptly dropped dead.

Ancient Greece

In terms of houseplant history, we owe much to the Greeks—more than to the Romans or even the Egyptians, if for no other reason than the wealth of early botanical art and literature that they left behind. Some of the first examples of true "houseplants" were recorded in the art of ancient Greece. After all, this was a civilization famous for decorating everything they touched, so it makes perfect sense that they would have ornamental plants and flowers. And the ancient Greek Theophrastus is considered, above anyone else, to be the father of botany.

Born in 371 BCE, Theophrastus went to Athens as a boy, where he studied under Plato. After Plato died, he transferred and began his studies with Aristotle at the Peripatetic school. Theophrastus became a very close friend and eventual colleague of Aristotle. In fact, he was Aristotle's successor when Aristotle left Athens in exile. He became the head of the Lyceum and proceeded to lead the Peripatetic school for thirty-six more years. During that time, he studied and wrote voluminously about botany.

While at the Lyceum, he wrote multiple volumes about his findings, the most important being *Enquiry into Plants*, which is also known as *Historia Plantarum*, and *On the Causes of Plants*. Most scholars consider these works to be the first botanical systems ever created, and the most important botanical writings until after the Middle Ages.

Historia Plantarum was written as ten books, but only nine have survived over the years. In the text, Theophrastus categorized more than four hundred plants by their natural locations, their sizes, and their uses.

Theophrastus's other work, *On the Causes of Plants*, was written as eight books, but only six have survived. The works describe how plants grow and exist in their habitats. Theophrastus described how to prep soil for planting, tools that one might need, and so on.

Theophrastus died in 287 BCE. His works were eventually translated into Arabic during the first year of the Common Era, and later into Latin and English. His body of work is the first instance of systemized organization of the botanical world. The surviving manuscripts were some of the most useful botanical resources during the Middle Ages.

Plants as Medicine

The ancient Greeks were brilliant physicians and were very keen to use what grew around them as remedies for various maladies. The dry Mediterranean climate was perfect for growing all kinds of herbs, which the ancient Greeks used medicinally. Here were a few of their favorites:

1. Mint
This herb was one of the most storied plants in all of Greek mythology and historical texts. It frequently comes up in mythological literature when Demeter, the goddess of agriculture, is mentioned. In ancient Greece, this herb was used for upset stomachs, halitosis, and insomnia.

2. Fennel
The Greeks prized fennel and used it often for all kinds of gut problems—from bloating to appetite issues.

3. Marsh Mallow
This isn't the soft, fluffy candy we're talking about here. I'm talking about marshmallow root, *Althea officinalis*. It was used, alongside fermented wine, to heal open wounds.

4. Peonies
The Balkan Peony, to be specific. This smaller variety was harvested for its roots and seeds. Ancient physicians used them to treat uterine issues, epilepsy, and other seizures. It's said that at the time, the demand was so high for the plant that physicians made up stories that the Balkan Peony could be deadly so they could scare off any potential peony poachers.

5. Licorice
This is one that had been used for 2,000 years before even the ancient Greeks were dabbling with it. We know now that licorice root is a noted antiviral, which explains why the Greeks would use it to treat asthma and pneumonia-like illnesses.

Myrtle + Pomegranate + Mythology: Two Plants We Keep as Houseplants Today

Myrtle

Myrtle is a plant that is beloved by topiary collectors. It's a small evergreen shrub that is aromatic and has deliciously spicy leaves. In the warmer months it blooms with sweet-smelling flowers and eventually produces edible black berries.

Many people keep their myrtle topiaries indoors year-round, but just as many put them outdoors during the summer. With the proper light exposure, a myrtle plant can thrive indoors for years.

The ancient Greeks were bonkers for myrtle. It was considered sacred to the goddess Aphrodite, so Greek brides wore garlands made of myrtle on their wedding day. They even took baths in myrtle-steeped water before getting hitched.

There seems to be a disturbing Greek myth to go along with every daily household object. Myrtle is no exception. The story goes that Myrrha, a Cyprian princess, fell in love with her father, King Theias (yikes!), and tried to seduce him while in disguise. After being found out, she ran away and was turned into a myrtle tree. As a tree, she gave birth to Adonis, the god of beauty and desire.

Native Habitat: *The Mediterranean regions and the Middle East*

The Pomegranate Tree

Over the years pomegranate trees—particularly the dwarf varieties—have become sought after by houseplant collectors. They will easily bear fruit, even indoors, under the proper care. The pomegranate tree is a deciduous (meaning it goes dormant and loses leaves annually) shrub that produces delicious red fruit about the size of an apple. Break the fruit open and you'll find seeds with a juicy, red pulp. This plant has been grown alongside apples, figs, and olives in the Mediterranean for thousands of years.

In Greek mythology, the pomegranate tree is the symbol of both Hera, wife of Zeus and the goddess of marriage, and Aphrodite, the goddess of love. The red, juicy seeds were a visual representation of female fertility. In the myth of Persephone, eating Hades's pomegranate seeds is what sealed her fate and forced her to spend half of every year in the underworld with him, ushering in winter. And the pomegranate is also featured in the myth of Orion's wife, Side. Side claimed that she was more beautiful than Hera, who, enraged, sent her down to Hades in the underworld, where she became a pomegranate tree.

Native Habitat: *The Middle East to northern India*

Ancient Rome

We like to blame the ancient Romans for lots of things. From modern traffic troubles (it's true!) to capital punishment and toxic politics, the ancient Romans kicked off a lot of bad societal habits. At its extremes, you could say that ancient Rome was violent and vile. However (you saw that coming, didn't you?), the Romans did have quite the eye for beauty.

Yes, the ancient Romans liked their pretty things, almost as much as the Greeks—and they were particularly fond of plants that flowered. Roses, marigolds, flowering bulbs, violets, and saffron were all popular picks of the time. Bonus points if the plants were imported from newly conquered lands in Egypt and Europe. Wealthy Romans grew them everywhere—inside their homes, villas, bathhouses, and courtyards and on palace facades. While terra-cotta was an option for pottery, the Romans preferred marble, even for their plants.

Like the Greeks and the Egyptians, the evidence of the ancient Romans' love for plants was left in both literature and in the ruins they left behind. Thanks to academics and archaeologists, we know what types of plants the Romans grew as well as how and why they found them useful enough to commit them to writing.

Up until just before the first century BCE, gardens were stunning, but were only appreciated for their utilitarian value. The vegetables, herbs, and flowers grown were used only for eating, treating maladies, and for religious ceremonies. Eventually, lilies, roses, and violets were grown to craft wreaths and sashes to decorate an outfit or a home for special occasions. Special urns and vessels were crafted for cut flowers to decorate homes as well as public spaces.

The practice of cultivating plants became highly sophisticated under the Roman thumb. Even though they would have likely dreaded to admit it, Roman gardening was heavily influenced by the Egyptians, Persians, and, yes, the Greeks.

If you examine Roman art and texts, you'll notice that a lot of these plants were kept in atriums or covered "outdoor" areas. Even though these spaces were technically outdoors, they were considered part of the living space. Many of these living spaces were filled with edible plants and flowers. Archaeological excavations have found planters and pots in the atriums of even the smallest homes.

The Gardens of Ancient Rome

Courtyard and atrium gardens were specially designed so that the plants could be seen from inside the home. Raised beds housed lilies, oleanders, stock, roses, and many other (generally tall) plants to be admired from indoors. These gardens frequently doubled as places of worship for people who lived there. Shrines to Roman gods and goddesses were found here—especially to Diana, Mars, and Minerva.

The Romans invented and constructed one of the first styles of unheated greenhouses. Greenhouses have been *essential* to the history of the care and keeping of plants in cultivation, and we have the ancient Romans to thank for them. All because a Roman emperor got sick.

In 30 CE, Emperor Tiberius became deathly ill and was told by his physician to eat one cucumber a day. Back then, it was no easy feat to have cucumbers readily available each and every day, all year long. Summer? No problem. Winter? That's a struggle. And so, the Roman greenhouse was invented.

There are a few accounts as to what this first actual greenhouse looked like. Up until this point, most of the plant-growing structures in Rome and Roman territories were called solariums or specularia. They were small structures where potted plants were housed in small boxes or rooms covered in transparent minerals like mica or selenite for protection. There are some records that state that some solariums were on wheels so that they could be moved along with the sun. The new, more permanent greenhouses were built with upgraded stone walls that worked as insulation and had transparent ceilings so that the cucumber plants could be exposed to as much light as possible.

Which visual account of the first greenhouse is actually correct? We don't know, but Tiberius did get his cucumbers year-round and lived to see a few more years.

Boxwood and Fennel

The best part about the Romans' passion for gardens is that it directly influenced Italian gardens and therefore Renaissance, baroque, and neoclassical garden designers. It would be easy to call this the golden age of garden design!

Two plants that the Romans loved—and that have remained hugely popular—are boxwoods and fennel.

Boxwoods

Okay, Romans weren't the "first" or "only" people to grow boxwoods or utilize their wood. Many civilizations that existed during the same time as ancient Rome used boxwood to make utensils, tablets, musical instruments, and jewelry boxes. The Egyptians also used boxwoods in their garden design. This wood is highly regarded not only for its strength but also for its flexibility.

These days boxwoods have become a staple in landscaping, but did you know that you can keep a boxwood indoors as a houseplant? Just like myrtle, boxwood is evergreen—meaning that it never sheds its leaves. Give it enough bright light and water regularly, and you'll be set. You can keep your boxwood in its natural shape, or you can trim it however you want.

Native Habitat: *Europe, Asia, and the Middle East*

Fennel

Fennel, *Foeniculum vulgare,* is one of the oldest plants in cultivation. Greeks used it mostly for medicines and remedies, and Romans absolutely loved it and used it in a variety of ways. In Roman mythology, the god Prometheus brought fire down from heaven and placed it on the stem of fennel. This herb, part of the carrot family, is one of the most versatile herbs on the planet. Romans used almost all parts of the plant: the seeds, the blossoms, and the leaves. Because of fennel's similarity to anise, it also quickly made its way into ancient Roman cuisine.

Pliny the Elder, the Roman author, naturalist, and philosopher, penned *Naturalis Historia* in 77 CE and referred to fennel multiple times. He cited it as a treatment for stomachache, snake bites, menstrual cramps, and various other afflictions. There is also evidence that a giant (now extinct) variety called silphium was used as an effective contraceptive.

Lucky for us modern-day folks, fennel is as easy to cultivate as it is to harvest. Maybe consider including it in your indoor herb garden.

Native Habitat: *Southern Europe and along the Mediterranean Sea*

YOUR LEAFY LEGACY:
Terra-Cotta 101

We know terra-cotta today as the material for the type of pot we buy when we want something easy and relatively inexpensive to put our plants in. Technically, terra-cotta ("baked earth" in Italian) is the name of all kinds of fired clay. Its texture is coarse and porous, and it is almost always left unglazed. The color is characteristically reddish-brown.

Many ancient civilizations utilized terra-cotta, specifically the Greeks, Egyptians, Romans, and Chinese. Greeks were using terra-cotta very early on, as early as the sixth century BCE, and the material eventually made its way to Egypt along with the ancient Greek people. In Egypt, the city of Alexandria turned terra-cotta into an industry. Terra-cotta was used to make figurines, statues, pottery, lamps, and more—they used terra-cotta for just about everything, even to make sarcophagi. The Romans mainly used terra-cotta in their architecture—they used terra-cotta tiles and bricks as building materials—and they also used it for decoration.

Garden Styles of Ancient Rome

Roman gardens were built around a variety of different locations and uses.

The Country Villa

Villas were used as "country" or weekend homes for the wealthy.

The Domus

This was a freestanding building that was publicly used for daily activities. It always had an atrium, where rainwater was collected. In the back was an open courtyard.

Palace Villa

This was the hub of the community, and the home of royalty.

Public Parks and Pleasure Gardens

These spaces included tombs, temples, and other public, nonresidential areas of the city.

Tenements

In small towns, there wasn't much space for plants and flowers. Occupants would plant flowers, veggies, and herbs in window boxes and pots on their roofs.

The Hortus

This is the word commonly used for "garden," but in this case it refers to a courtyard in the back of a private residence used to grow vegetables and herbs. It was practical and not ornamental.

In China, makers and artisans used terra-cotta regularly. Perhaps in the most famous example, thousands of life-size terra-cotta warriors were crafted for the first Qin emperor, Qin Shi Huang. Historians believe they were created between 247 and 208 BCE for the emperor's self-built mausoleum. The First Emperor was obsessed with the idea of the afterlife, so much so that he created an entire terra-cotta army to escort him there after death.

YOUR LEAFY LEGACY:
The Best Houseplants Suited for Terra-Cotta

Terra-cotta pottery has always been one of the most popular options for keeping houseplants. It makes an affordable, sustainable, long-lasting pottery that can be found in any garden shop.

One of the best things about terra-cotta is that it's a porous material that lets oxygen and moisture pass between the interior and exterior of the container. This lets the soil dry from all angles, instead of from the top down, which is wonderful because it prevents all kinds of nasty problems like root rot and fungi. There's no easier pot to manage than a terra-cotta pot, and that makes them great for beginning houseplant collectors.

There are, of course, a few downsides to terra-cotta. Some popular houseplants like Alocasias and Calatheas need help retaining moisture—so porous terra-cotta isn't the best option. And because terra-cotta is so porous, moisture wicks out, which can easily damage whatever surface the pot is sitting on. So be sure to set your pot on a coaster or get felt feet for it from your local garden center or hardware store.

Some plants just work better in terra-cotta than others! Here's a starter pack of terra-cotta-loving plants:

Citrus

Many people who keep citrus trees as houseplants choose to grow them in terra-cotta pots because they help to dry out the soil evenly. Citrus plants do not like to sit in wet or damp soil for long periods of time, so terra-cotta is a great option for them!

Citrus plants need bright light, warm temperatures, and minimal water to thrive and produce fruit. Lemons, mandarins, kumquats, and pomegranates are great starter houseplant citrus.

Native Habitat: *Citrus plants are mainly native to subtropical and tropical regions of Asia and northern Australia.*

Ponytail Palm

Beaucarnea recurvata
Ponytail Palms are a great drought-tolerant option if you're looking for a plant with green leaves and a ton of sass. The caudex, or expanded stem, funnels into a narrow trunk that erupts in green, wispy leaves that almost look like hair. As a houseplant, they rarely reach more than four feet tall and grow very slowly. They need bright light, warm temperatures, and minimal water to thrive.

Native Habitat: *Mexico, Belize, and Guatemala*

String of Pearls

Senecio rowleyanus
One of the best ways to get this plant to produce long strands of those gorgeous pearl-like leaves is to keep it in a terra-cotta pot. There is much debate among houseplant enthusiasts, but the porous material keeps the roots from getting waterlogged.

This plant prefers to be root bound—when a plant's root density takes up the entire pot—and can grow slowly if not allowed to grow into its pot.

Like most plants on this list, it needs bright light and minimal water.

Native Habitat: *Southwestern Africa*

Swiss Cheese Plant

Monstera deliciosa

The monstera is one of the most popular houseplants on the market for good reason, and this isn't the first or last time it will be recommended in this book. It's easy to grow as a houseplant, and it's just wonderful to look at with its big, fenestrated leaves. Even better, this plant grows great in affordable terra-cotta. While monsteras aren't quite as drought tolerant as other plants on this list, they are forgiving if you forget to give them a drink.

Monsteras enjoy indirect light and water when their soil starts to dry out, so you might find yourself watering one a little more often than if it were planted in a glazed pot, but that's okay. Monsteras like the attention—and you'll have more opportunities to appreciate those huge, glowing leaves.

Native Habitat: *Central America*

Herbs

There are many, many herbs out there, and most perform wonderfully in terra-cotta pots. Rosemary, mint, oregano, and thyme are great options and prefer the airiness around their roots that terra-cotta can provide.

When grown indoors, herbs need bright light and must be watered when the soil is dry to the touch.

Native Habitat: *Rosemary—Mediterranean*
Mint—Temperate areas of the world
Oregano—Mediterranean
Thyme—Europe and Asia

YOUR LEAFY LEGACY:
Your Plants Outside

During the warmer months of the year, the sun is hot, the weather slightly unpredictable, and gardens are in full swing. Outdoor plants are thriving, while our houseplants may be looking longingly out the window, dreaming of time spent in the sunshine.

Okay, yes, the idea is a bit campy, but our houseplants are indeed wild things that have a native habitat *outdoors*. When it warms up and the fear of freezing temps is gone, it's the perfect time to place your houseplants outside if you have the space. Time outside can be a great motivator that promotes new growth and the overall health of your plants. If done correctly, moving your houseplants outdoors will usually help promote blooming. But there are many things to be conscious of when you're bringing your indoor friends outside to play. This is not a beginner houseplant parent move. It requires you to be aware of the weather and your plant's condition at all times. The elements can wreak havoc on houseplants very quickly. Wind, rain, and heat can kill a houseplant in less than a day if you're not careful.

Heat

If you're an urban gardener, then you're surrounded by concrete and asphalt, which absorbs heat from the sun at an alarming rate. The air might only be 75 degrees Fahrenheit, but any plants on concrete or asphalt will feel like it's over 100 degrees. Usually your plants are much closer to the ground, so they will catch the radiating heat much faster than you will. Even if you're not an urban gardener, the sun will dry out plants much faster when they're outside.

Rain and Inclement Weather

A good storm can tear a houseplant to pieces because their roots aren't anchored in the ground. Also, if your pot has no drainage, there is a risk of overwatering.

Wind

A nice breeze won't hurt. But consistent, strong gusts can topple your plants and wick the moisture away from the roots before you even realize that it's windy outside.

Look at the Temperatures

Just because your local nurseries are starting to sell summer annuals doesn't mean that it's warm enough at night for most plants to survive, especially houseplants. To be safe, wait a month after the last frost to even consider putting houseplants outside. Some advice out there says that your plants will be okay once the nighttime temperature is consistently above 55 degrees Fahrenheit. Wait until it's consistently above 60 degrees.

Check Your Pot Situation

It is very important that your houseplant be potted in a container that has drainage before you put it outside. This not only can help you regulate watering but also can prevent the plant from drowning if you leave it out during a downpour.

Watch for Bugs

Once you bring your indoor plants outside, they become susceptible to all the creatures that live outdoors. It's a good idea to give those plants a once-over every day or two just to see if anything is eating them and if any bugs have moved in. You might want to be ready with insecticidal soap just in case those slugs try to get the best of you and your plant.

Placement Matters

Do not place your houseplants in a spot that gets direct sun for most of the day (or, in some cases, for more than five hours). Even if the plant is a succulent or cactus, it will not be used to that much exposure and will get a sunburn. Always put your plants where they are in partial shade for most of the day, just to be safe.

Water

Gardeners lose more houseplants outside to under-watering than anything else. You must make sure that your plants are watered every day, whether by rain or by hose/watering can. The plants will dry out faster than you think they will! Check and then check again. When temperatures are warmer, it's best to water outdoor plants either first thing in the morning or in the early evening. You want to ensure your plants will have enough moisture to get them through the stress of a hot day.

CHAPTER 3

Itty Bitty Mini-Gardens

THE HAN DYNASTY AND THE INTRODUCTION OF PENJING (220)

It is one thing to be a houseplant connoisseur, but it's another thing altogether to be a master of meticulously and artfully shaped, minuscule, delicate plants. Hundreds of years before the art of bonsai came on the scene, the Chinese were sculpting trees into miniature works of art. Somewhere around 220 BCE, a Taoist monk plunked a dwarf tree foraged from the wild into a shallow tray and successfully kept it alive.

Taoists of the time believed that re-creating aspects of nature in miniature form could force positive energy back into nature and allow it to thrive. The practice then spread to Japan and Vietnam over the next thousand years.

Penjing

These containers of carefully pruned trees were created as mini landscapes. The container was called the pen and was traditionally a shallow bowl with feet. It could be made of various materials, but only the most beautiful containers made of bronze were used in religious and official ceremonies.

Around the first century CE and into the second, Taoist and Buddhist teachings focused on re-creating nature in miniature, and creating and maintaining penjing became a common religious practice in many parts of China. Penjing pots adorned homes, temples, and public spaces. Many of the landscapes were created with rocks, pebbles, and dwarfed fruit trees. The most prized of all the penjing were the wild trees that had been collected from the forest and were physically imperfect. It was said that these old, deformed trees carried ancient energy. Younger plants were also collected, and monks used intricate techniques to train them to eventually achieve the look of those oldest wild trees.

Today, the art of penjing is still used to tell a story through the contrasts of texture, materials, and place. You'll find penjing that mimic an outdoor garden just on the other side of a door as part of a larger garden design concept. And they're often perched on a bookshelf, coffee table, or other accented platform—merging interior design with nature.

Hòn Non Bộ

Hòn Non Bộ is the Vietnamese practice of making miniature landscapes, like the Chinese practice of penjing. Over time, as the art of penjing spread across Asia, each country where it took hold adapted the art based on the traditions and the religious needs of its people. While penjing deals with miniature landscapes, mostly made of rocks and trees harvested from nature, Hòn Non Bộ takes it to the next level.

The Vietnamese practice imitates specific landscapes—for example, a particular island or mountain, or just the artist's surroundings. Hòn Non Bộ tend to be larger than penjing and bonsai but can sometimes be very small and straightforward. The best part is that they almost always involve a water feature.

After all, it's all in the name:

Hòn—Island
Non—Mountain
Bộ—Water, mountains, and trees, or simply "miniature scenes"

Traditionally, Hòn Non Bộ were built for the upper class of Vietnamese society and were displayed in the courtyards of homes, so they were the first thing seen upon entering the property, to establish the esteem of the owner.

Bonsai

So, what exactly is the difference between penjing, Hòn Non Bộ, and bonsai?

Both penjing and Hòn Non Bộ seek to create entire scenes—exact replicas of places you can see in nature in miniature. Bonsai, on the other hand, is solely sculpting trees into a certain form and shape. No scenes, just trees.

It started after the art of penjing traveled to Japan with monks who had been in China. They brought back penjing pots and stories of how Taoists and Buddhists created the miniature scenes. The art form took off, propelled by popular culture of the time, and eventually adapted to Japanese tastes, becoming the related art of bonsai.

Hachi no Ki, translated as "The Potted Trees," is a 1383 Noh play by Zeami Motokiyo. The famous play tells the story of a poor samurai who sets fire to his last three potted trees for firewood to help warm up a monk who is passing through during the winter. The monk, who is actually a government official in disguise, rewards the samurai for his help. The potted trees that are referenced in the play were dwarf trees that were planted in the penjing style. The play became hugely popular, which led many Japanese artists to depict its scenes through various mediums like tapestries and prints. Kind of like modern-day fan art.

Century by century, the art of bonsai grew more popular. By the seventeenth century, it was thoroughly embedded into Japanese culture. By the nineteenth century, bonsai had spread westward. At the beginning of the twentieth century, global interest in bonsai came with the increased arbor trade along with global interest in foreign cultures. Japan hosted multiple international bonsai shows before World War II to great success. Tokyo's three hundred bonsai dealers were cranking out more than 150 species in cultivation that were shipped all over the world before the war brought the trade screeching to a halt.

The craft has bounced back in the Western world. Now there are thousands of bonsai apprentices worldwide. The oldest bonsai still living today has been dated all the way back to 1610. This tree, named Sandai-Shogun-No Matsu, resides in the Tokyo Imperial Palace's private collection.

Bonsai is a compelling, complicated practice that is frequently misunderstood. A lot of the time it is confused with dwarfing a plant, but it's not even close to that. Dwarfing is a process of miniaturizing an existing species by selective breeding and genetic mutations. Instead, bonsai strictly uses cultivation techniques like pruning, wiring, and root modification to produce a tree that copies the look and feel of a full-size specimen.

It should be noted that traditionally bonsai does not include the practice of keeping a tree indoors. Tropical bonsai is a relatively new thing compared with the age of the practice. Almost all professional bonsai that you see in botanic gardens, shows, and collections have been grown outdoors.

Bonsai symbolize harmony, peace, and the balance of life, as well as everything that is good in nature. The practice is just as important as the finished product—which is the main reason why bonsai is such a widely appreciated and important art form.

YOUR LEAFY LEGACY:
Bonsai 101

The word "bonsai" is translated to "tree in a pot." Literally. And that's exactly what bonsai is—a common tree or shrub that has been cultivated and pruned and groomed into a specific shape. These trees will go through the seasons and flower, produce fruit, and drop leaves if the plant is deciduous. If you have a tropical plant or tree, it will stay green for you all year long.

One thing that is important to understand is that bonsai is a learned art in patience and appreciation for the tree you're working with. It's not a craft you can just pick up in an afternoon and expect immediate success. The purpose of bonsai isn't what the tree will produce for you. Instead, it's about the process and focus that it takes to coax a plant into long-term cultivation in a small container. The goal is to create a bonsai that looks like a tree that has been growing in nature and has been exposed to all the elements of the wild world. There is no official end point; it's a continuous labor of love and meditation.

There are tools and skills you'll need if you want to try your hand at bonsai. Here's a brief how-to, just so you can whet your appetite. If you're interested in diving deep, purchase a bonsai guide and sign up for a class at a local plant shop or botanic garden.

There are specific bonsai tools out there for purchase, but for your first foray into bonsai they're not 100 percent necessary. Concave pruners, root hooks, and bud scissors are all designed for more precise cuts in cramped, small spaces. If you're just using bonsai scissors or a small pair of cutters, be careful and take your time. Don't rush the process!

You'll need:

- A starter plant
- Ceramic bonsai container
- A shallow tray
- Pebbles or small rocks
- Bonsai soil
- Copper wire (Remember, if you're going to wire your plant, take it off if you notice it cutting into the trunk or branch over time.)
- Bonsai scissors
- Wire cutters
- Rubbing alcohol—to clean your tools

Before you get started, consider the following:

Picking a starter plant

Generally speaking, starting an indoor bonsai with a tropical plant is the easiest because of the semitropical temperatures in our homes. Varieties of ficus species tend to be great starter plants because of their resilience. Many people also start with bougainvillea and *Serissa japonica*.

As easy as it is these days to order your starter plant online, head over to your favorite garden center and start your search there. If you do take your search online, look for reputable bonsai growers.

If you purchase a temperate tree instead of a tropical one, be ready to keep it outdoors. Temperate bonsai will struggle in an indoor setting. Stick with subtropical and tropical species for indoor bonsai.

Soil

Bonsai soil is a well-draining soil, and it's important to use this type of mix. Regular potting soil will likely induce root rot because it will hold far more water than your plant will need. Buy the right mix at the outset and save yourself the future trouble and heartache of a rotting root system. You can find it at just about any garden center or online retailer that sells potting mixes. There are even different kinds for different types of bonsai (tropical, temperate, etc.).

You should only have to repot your bonsai every two to three years.

Water

Like other houseplants, your bonsai will have a growing season and a more dormant season in the cooler months. During the warmer growing months, keep your plant moist (not soaking) at all times. If you have naturally dry air in your home, you might want to consider investing in a small humidifier to keep the air around your bonsai humid enough. In the winter, water only when the surface of the soil is dry to the touch, but don't let it dry out completely.

Light

Tropical bonsai need a significant amount of light and will perform best in a west- or south-facing window. Of course, if you're in a pinch, grow lights will help supplement the light in your home. Many bonsai owners put their tropical plants outdoors in the warmer months—but remember to acclimate them!

Alright, are you ready to give it a try?

Root and Crown Pruning

In order for your bonsai to have a healthy growing pattern, you'll need to prune both the roots and the crown of your plant.

1. Roots

Prune back one-third of the roots every repotting so that new soil can be added to the container. Without space and new soil, the plant will drain the nutrients from the soil. Root pruning also allows for new root growth to emerge.

2. Crown

You must keep the trunk line visible at all times. This is the most important part! Instead of cutting all low branches without thought, first think about what branches you want to accentuate, and then decide which ones to remove. Keep only the branches that grow on the curve of the trunk.

It's important to remember the rule of thirds. Don't prune off more than one-third of the plant at a time, or it will suffer and potentially die.

Bonsai Design Styles

There are a few popular styles that are considered typical bonsai: upright, informal upright, slanting, cascade, and semicascade.

Upright

Make sure one-third of the trunk is visible from the front. Branches always follow a pattern. The first branch from the bottom is the longest and trained to grow one-third of the height of the tree, making a right angle to the trunk. The second branch is opposite the first and higher on the trunk, and so on. The branches go up the trunk and taper into a cone-like appearance with thick foliage at the top so that you can't see the branches or trunk. Some branches lean forward at the top toward the front of the plant.

Informal upright

Same as above, but a little wilder. The trunk is still tapered, but the position and branches look more like they've been out in the elements than with a perfectly pruned tree. The trunk curves around with the branches somewhat balanced on each side. The crown of the tree is flush. Many folks use jin, the art of carving unwanted bonsai branches to look like dead parts of a tree, for this style of bonsai.

Slanting

This is similar to the informal upright style. The trunk can be straight or curved, but it has to angle either to the left or the right. Never toward the front. The center of the tree should never be directly over the base of the tree. To get the trunk to angle in a certain direction, you'll need to wire it while it's young. You can also get the trunk to curve by placing the pot on a slanted surface.

Cascade

This style requires the tip of the bonsai to grow downward toward the bottom of the pot. The trunk is trained with wire to twist down below the side of the container, which makes the bonsai look like it's being pulled downward. A tall, narrow pot is useful to achieve this style. The trunk will need to be wired to pull down over the line of the container with a major focal point in the bend. Keep the branches the same and vertical to the trunk. Make sure to position the tree in the center of the pot.

Semicascade

Similar to the cascade—obviously—but without such an obvious angle or bend in the trunk, just a little bit downward.

It can be difficult to decide when a branch should be cut. Should you keep it or cut it? Here are some tips on when to make the cut:

- 🖉 when there are two branches at the same height on the trunk;
- 🖉 when you have a wonky, weird branch;
- 🖉 when there are thick branches at the top of the tree.

Where to see amazing bonsai, penjing, and Hòn Non Bộ

What: *The National Bonsai & Penjing Museum*
Where: *Washington, DC*
Notable: *Its collection has more than 150 plants*

What: *Master Kobayashi's eight-hundred-year-old bonsai*
Where: *Shunkaen Bonsai Museum, Tokyo, Japan*
Notable: *Master Kunio Kobayashi has won the distinguished Prime Minister's Award for Bonsai four times.*

What: *Goshin, a forest planting of eleven junipers, the oldest of which was planted in 1948*
Where: *United States National Arboretum, Washington, DC*
Notable: *Created by John Y. Naka, who donated it to the National Bonsai Foundation in 1984*

What: *Omiya Bonsai Village*
Where: *Saitama, Japan*
Notable: *The village is essentially a large collection of bonsai nurseries that all relocated from Tokyo after a massive earthquake in 1923. There is also a fantastic bonsai art museum on site.*

CHAPTER 4

Gardening for Prudes

THE MIDDLE AGES (500–1453)

All good things must come to an end. The Roman Empire began its downward slide in the year 350 CE, and with it fell the frivolous horticultural status symbol. In the West during this time, ornamental plants took a back seat to their traditional, utilitarian cousins. This state of affairs carried on through the Crusades and the Middle Ages. Bor-ing!

It hurts the heart to think of how many plants in cultivation were lost during this time, but this chapter will show you how to handle yourself when it seems like your own precious houseplants are dying. It'll also teach you about utilitarian crops that can be grown indoors with a primer on how to grow plants like ginger, microgreens, and herbs inside your house. It'll even cover a few mystical, medicinal plants as well.

Grab your lantern and your pitchfork—and let's go!

Inside the Middle Ages

Long story short is that the civilization of Rome fell to Germanic tribes in the fifth century CE, which ushered in the Middle Ages, the first half of which is commonly known as the Dark Ages. From roughly 500 to 1500 CE, Western Europe descended into a period of intellectual darkness. It wasn't until around 1600 that any cultural evidence had been found about the use of plants in the home.

All of this is a shame, of course—developments in the humanities and sciences screeched to a halt and didn't start to move forward again until well into the 1500s. Technically you could count the slow progression of important Roman and Greek texts being translated into Latin about 500 years in as a positive cultural development. But even crediting that, during this period the progression of Western civilization moved at a snail's pace and received massive pushback from the Roman Catholic Church.

The center of the universe (aka the Byzantine Empire) had moved from Rome to Constantinople, an act which allowed the Roman Catholic Church to gain massive, sweeping power over the entirety of Western Europe. The empire changed its official religion to Christianity and its official language from Latin to Greek. From that point forward, until the 1500s, any view different from the church was deemed heresy and punishable by death.

Economic and living conditions were so awful that the cumulative effort of society was put into surviving another day. Not many people were interested in keeping plants in their homes for sport until living conditions improved in the mid-1500s.

Everything grown during this time had to have a practical use. When Pliny the Elder's *Naturalis Historia* was finally translated to Latin in the 1400s, his ideas put fuel on the fire of the utilitarian plant ideology. Other guides—called "herbals"—available at the time included a work by Dioscórides, a Greek physician who had written about 500 plants used for medicines.

Monasteries sat at the center of the medieval food and medicine chains. They cultivated gardens that provided crops and medicinal plants to their communities by order of the government and royal houses. These gardens frequently included orchards, fishponds, and raised garden beds, and they were surrounded by fences for protection from unsavory or desperate folks who might feel the urge to steal. While vegetables were grown in these gardens, there was a large focus on multiuse herbs, like rosemary, sage, and lavender, which were somewhat easy to grow.

After the Crusades came to an end around 1291, Asian spices like ginger, nutmeg, and cardamom became available and somewhat accessible for the wealthy and the members of royal families.

This is a great spot to stop and point out that even if people wanted to bring plants indoors during the Dark Ages, it would've been extremely difficult to keep anything alive. It's also called the Dark Ages for a literal reason! Indoor spaces were cold, dark, and damp. Even the castles and large homes built for royalty were cavernous inside. Carpets and tapestries covered the walls and were prized—never to be stepped on—so the floors mostly remained uncovered and chilly. Windows were small, and decorative extravagances were left for the church, not for the home. If you wanted light, you had to go outside.

Medicinal Plants of the Dark Ages

Medicines in the Dark Ages were made of herbs, spices, and resins that were rooted in antiquated Greek medical knowledge. A monastery's herb garden was referred to as an "infirmary herb garden" and was maintained by a monk who specialized in medicinal plants. These infirmary gardens were quite rare, as most gardens were multiuse and not completely dedicated to medicinal herbs. There were a few monasteries, however, like the Rievaulx Abbey in Yorkshire, England, that had an entire garden dedicated to medicine. Monasteries with these gardens were often located in heavily populated areas and had many sick people to care for.

Medieval medicine was crude. Commonly used medical practices were based on the four "humors" of the body, which were related to the four elements: air, water, fire, and earth. If there was phlegm, it was related to water and therefore cold and damp. Blood related to air and was hot and damp. The biles, yellow and black, related to fire and earth, respectively, and were hot (yellow), cold (black), and dry.

In order to heal a patient's ailment, physicians believed they had to restore the balance in the body systems. Each medicinal plant used had specific properties that were purported to align with the elements. If you had too much black bile (cold), a warming herb would be used, and so on.

Here's a look at a few of the most popular medieval herbs that made many appearances in records throughout the era.

Rose

Rose was used for the common prevention of scurvy. Combined with oil or vinegar, it was used to reduce or cure headaches and earaches, among other maladies.

Native Habitat: *Central Asia, Europe, North America, and northwestern Africa*

Lavender

Lavender was used for heart pains, fainting spells, restlessness, epilepsy, kidney issues, and headaches. It was also used topically for various bites.

Native Habitat: *Europe, northeastern Africa, the Mediterranean, and Asia*

Sage

Sage was used against various bites and maladies that came from lack of hygiene. It was also chewed, along with mint, to whiten teeth and freshen breath.

Native Habitat: *The Mediterranean but now naturalized in Europe and North America*

Wormwood

Wormwood, also the psychedelic ingredient in absinthe, was frequently used to cure fevers and headaches. Lights out!

Native Habitat: *Europe, Africa, and Asia*

Mint

Various mints were used to treat venomous bites and festering wounds. It was also used, along with sage, to keep breath fresh and teeth white. It was frequently used in oils and vinegars as well.

Native Habitat: *Temperate areas of the world*

Comfrey

Comfrey was used to wrap open wounds and around a limb with a broken bone. It was commonly known as the "knit" herb because of its high level of allantoin, which promotes cell proliferation and helps to heal busted bones and broken skin faster than letting time run its course.

Native Habitat: *England, Europe, Asia, and Siberia*

Licorice

Licorice was used to treat asthma, sore throats, and all kinds of ulcers. Some physicians even doled it out for help with fertility issues.

Native Habitat: *Asia, North Africa, and Europe*

Hyssop

Hyssop was the cold remedy drug of the time. It combatted snotty noses and phlegmy chests.

Native Habitat: *Europe and North America*

Lungwort

As the name suggests, lungwort was used against inflamed lungs and bouts of severe coughing. Unfortunately, it is also poisonous and causes liver damage.

Native Habitat: *Europe and western Asia*

Chamomile

Chamomile was used as a calming sedative for both the head and the digestive system. It was also frequently used as a (somewhat successful) antidote to many poisons.

Native Habitat: *Europe, Africa, and Asia*

Betony

Of all the herbs in the medieval book of herbal cures, betony was one of the most popular, and was used to treat just about every ailment and then some—even fear and anger.

Native Habitat: *Europe and North America*

YOUR LEAFY LEGACY:
Cold Houseplants? Don't Panic! (Yet)

Even though we don't plan for our houseplants to get cold, sometimes it happens. The best method for protecting houseplants in the cold is to implement preventive measures. Make sure your windows are sealed and closed properly and you've moved all your plants away from chilly drafts and cold windowpanes. Keep those houseplants away from doors that open to the outside. But what exactly do you do if you forget to pull your plants in off the sun porch after a sunny early spring day, and then it freezes overnight?

It's not guaranteed that they'll recover, but don't give up hope. If your plants are suffering because they have been exposed to cold temperatures, they could still make a comeback.

You have to remember that most common houseplants are tropical, and a lot of them are extremely sensitive to temperatures under 50 degrees Fahrenheit. Some will start dying the second the temps dip, but others can regenerate from healthy roots below the soil, even if the top part of the plant is completely frozen. Another important factor is how long the plants were exposed to cold temperatures. A few hours can do the job, depending on the plant. Generally, though, it takes twelve to twenty-four hours to completely kill most tropical plant species all the way through the roots.

If you're in doubt, check the roots. If they're white and firm, that's a good sign. If they're mushy, there's no hope. As always, there's the possibility that the roots are somewhere in between, and if that's the case, you should give revival a chance with the following tips.

1. Bring the plant into a warmer area as soon as possible. Don't go about cutting off any foliage that looks dead; simply concentrate on getting the plant warm. The recovery process will start (depending on the length of cold exposure) as soon as it warms up. Don't try to accelerate the process by placing it on a radiator or heating element. Let it happen naturally through exposure to the warmer environment.

2. Water the plant right away with a small quantity and let it drain out of the container. When plants freeze, the moisture gets sucked from the leaf tissue, so give it a drink. As the plant tries to recover, water as you normally would.

3. Do not fertilize.

4. Cut off all dead blooms and foliage after the plant has been "warm" for at least a month. The plant needs to regenerate energy, so give it some time.

You'll know if the plant is completely dead if you leave it alone for a month or two and it does not begin to show signs of new growth. With plants, you win some and you lose some. The longer you garden or keep a houseplant collection, the more you'll learn.

YOUR LEAFY LEGACY:
Microgreens 101

Who says houseplants can't be utilitarian? And, who says you can't grow edible greens indoors? You can grow enormous helpings of microgreens right in your kitchen window in an upcycled takeout container. Doesn't that sound like the best idea ever? Sure, you can buy microgreens at any grocery store, but growing them in your home is even easier than a quick trip to the store.

Delicious, crunchy microgreens have been wildly popular for years. Common varieties of microgreens include basil, beets, broccoli, kale, peas, and cabbage. They are the itty-bitty leaves of these veggies that are harvestable once the germinated seeds have sprouted.

Microgreens are extremely quick and simple to grow, with some varieties ready to harvest in just one week. They are also cost-effective and nutrient dense. With a little practice, you'll find that you spend less time and money growing your own microgreens than buying them packaged at the store.

I know what you're thinking. "What she's saying is great, except I don't have the space for a veggie garden in my house!" But guess what? All you need to grow your own microgreens is a small, shallow container, some potting mix, water, and good light.

Now wait

You will need a shallow container that's a couple of inches deep (this is the perfect reuse for that plastic takeout container), seeds, seed-starting mix, and a spray bottle. If you want organic microgreens, make sure all your products are organic, even the soil. Everything counts.

Prep your seeds

If you've chosen larger seeds (peas, wheat, sunflowers, etc.) you'll need to soak them overnight before planting them. This helps with the germination process.

Get your soil ready

Fill your chosen container three-quarters full with your potting mix. You should have at least one inch of mix to work with. Mist or dampen your soil. Push it around so that you have an even layer in your container.

Plant!

Sprinkle your seeds generously over the soil. Use your hand to gently press them down into the potting mix. Mist thoroughly! Don't water with a watering can; you'll move the seeds around in the mix, and they won't germinate as well for you.

Now wait

Place the tray in a warm, sunny spot. Warm and sunny is key. If you don't have a warm or sunny spot but still want to grow microgreens, invest in a small heating mat and a grow light.

If you have a sunny spot but are worried about humidity, upcycle a plastic shopping bag. Cut a few small holes in it and put your tray inside, creating your own little greenhouse.

Keep the soil moist, but not soaking. Overwater and you'll have drowned seeds. Just as with your houseplants, touch the soil with your fingertips to test for moisture before watering.

Harvest and enjoy

After your seedlings hit about one to two inches tall, they'll be ready to harvest. You can also judge this by how many leaves they've put out. After they've produced two leaves, they're ready.

Grab a pair of scissors and cut the stems right up to the soil. Rinse any potting mix off your microgreens, put those puppies on a plate, and enjoy!

Troubleshooting

Yes, growing microgreens at home can be quick and easy, but that doesn't mean you can't run into a few hiccups. There are many different variations to the above steps, so modify at your leisure. Some folks like to use containers with drainage, and some don't. Some give their germinating seeds "blackout" time before putting them in the light, and some don't. Growing microgreens is an affordable, easy hobby that is easily tinkerable to your needs. Mess around with the process and go with what works best for you.

Here are some possible issues you could run into:

Mold

Mold and microgreens sometimes go hand in hand. This is because wet soil plus humidity equals a prime mold-growing environment.

To prevent it, make sure your seed tray is in a well-ventilated area. If you're using a covering, make sure air is allowed to flow over the tray. Good ventilation will prevent a majority of mold problems.

Mold can sometimes look like root hairs. Here's how to tell the difference: Mold will look like a silky spiderweb, while root hairs look fuzzy. You'll also find that root hairs will turn down and disappear when watered; mold will not. If you touch mold, it will be slimy, sticky, and carry a stale, musty aroma; root hairs will not.

If you find yourself with a mold issue, it's generally easier to scrap the batch, change out the soil, and try again. If you don't want to give up, make a mixture of water (½), hydrogen peroxide (¼), and vinegar (¼). Spray on your microgreens and the mold. It should kill the mold growing on your plants, but once you harvest the greens, wash them thoroughly to make sure no remainder of mold is left behind. (PS: This tip works for mold growing in any type of houseplant!) Put the tray in bright sunlight. Mold hates sunlight. Just make sure you don't let your greens dry out in the sun.

Yellow Stems and Leaves

When most microgreens shoot through the soil, they're yellow in color. This is simply because the chlorophyll inside the leaves hasn't had a chance to photosynthesize. Once they get enough light, they'll turn the appropriate color.

Leggy Stems

If your microgreens are becoming leggy and weak stemmed, they aren't getting enough light. If they continue to stretch, the greens will eventually collapse because they will have spent all their energy. Give your microgreens more light, and they should self-correct.

YOUR LEAFY LEGACY:
Grow Your Own Ginger, as a Houseplant!

Ginger ale, ginger snaps, ginger chews, and ginger beer. The zing that zips through your senses when you pop a ginger treat in your mouth is hard to beat. The ancient root, native to China, is one of the most utilitarian spices known to man. And—surprise—you can grow it in your home!

The rhizome, or root of the plant, is what is commonly known as ginger, and it is closely related to turmeric. It can be used fresh, dried, candied, powdered, or juiced. It has been widely utilized medicinally for all kinds of ailments. If you're feeling under the weather for any variety of reasons, chances are ginger can give you a boost. It's a wonderful anti-nausea and anti-inflammatory agent, which is why it has been known as a "miracle drug" for centuries, including in the Middle Ages.

However you like it, in the kitchen or in the medicine cabinet, it's an easy plant to grow. Yes, it's a breeze to grow outdoors, but it's a fun and educational experience to grow it indoors in a container! Even though ginger can be slow to sprout, follow these simple steps and you'll be harvesting your own ginger before you know it.

Get Your Ginger

Whether you snag a chunk from a friend or buy it from the grocery store, you'll need a smallish piece of ginger that's at least the size of your thumb. Make sure it has nodes or protrusions—this is where the roots will sprout out of later on. Your ginger also needs to be nice and plump. Shriveled or old pieces will not sprout.

Also, you will need to scrub the piece of root with hot water and a mild soap. This is particularly true if you have purchased the ginger from a grocery store and it is not organic. Like other root veggies, they are sprayed with a substance that prevents them from rotting on the shelves of the store. If the spray is not scrubbed off, the rhizome will not root for you.

Sprouting with Patience

For this step you're going to create a controlled growing space for your ginger. You will need a sealable container, like a Tupperware or plastic takeout container.

Fill your container halfway with potting mix. Next, nestle the ginger down into the soil and cover it with a thin layer of the mix. Water the soil so that it is damp all the way through, but not soggy. Ginger that sits in wet, soggy potting mix will rot, not sprout.

Put the lid on the container, but do not seal it. Place it somewhere warm and in indirect light. Check the soil every week or so, watering it when it looks dry.

You should see sprouts within six to eight weeks. It's a bit of a wait, but the payoff is worth it!

Plant

Once your little nugget of ginger has sprouts of its own, it will be time to repot! Once sprouted, ginger grows rapidly and will need a larger container. Drainage is a must. If your ginger rhizomes sit in water, they will surely rot, and you'll be back to square one.

Fill your new, large pot with potting mix. Bury your sprouted ginger in the top four inches of the soil, with the sprouts exposed. Water thoroughly!

You'll want to put the container in a sunny window and give it lots of water. Over time you will notice the rhizome, what looks like the root of the plant, will break the surface of the soil. Keep tabs on it and make sure to cover it up with new soil as it appears. Rhizomes that remain exposed will turn green and tough.

Harvest

Even though ginger can grow at a rapid pace in the perfect conditions, it's likely that your ginger won't be ready for harvest until six to eight months after repotting. Just be patient. Start that crafting project you've always wanted to try. Finish writing that novel you've been working on. Expand your houseplant collection. Anything to give your ginger time to populate its container.

Finally, the time will come to harvest!

If you want to harvest smaller pieces for everyday use, dig around gently with your fingers and uncover a rhizome. Use a sharp knife or pair of scissors to cut off what you need, and then cover the rhizome again.

If you need a lot of ginger, simply pull the root up by the stalk and cut it off.

The most important thing to remember is to not overharvest. You will need to leave at least a third of the ginger rhizome attached to the stalk in order for it to continue growing. If you treat your rhizomes correctly, you can grow ginger this way until the end of time.

CHAPTER 5

The Time When Columbus Kick-Started Botanical Imperialism

(1492–1650)

"In 1492, Columbus sailed the ocean blue." And then he did a few other things that, even by the standards of his own time, made him widely despised. His inhumanity is well documented, and while the purpose here is not to drag him through the mud (though he'd deserve it), Christopher Columbus and the Columbian Exchange were responsible for the worldwide spread of botany and other "products" from one part of the world to another.

The Renaissance, including the rebirth of the artistic world, was booming during Columbus's time, and along with it came the resurgence of indoor cultivars. This comeback was aided by the acquisition of plants by explorers. For hundreds of years adventurers traversed the globe, digging up exotic plants, tossing them in crates, and shipping them back to Europe. These new, alien plants titillated the interest of many scholars and scientists, but most importantly they piqued the interest of royalty, whose appetites and coffers fueled even more botanical exploration.

When Christopher Columbus Changed Everything

Ah, Christopher Columbus, the famous Italian explorer who rocked so many boats that his entire "legacy" is up for debate. Most schoolchildren in the United States were taught about how Columbus discovered America in the name of the Spanish crown and paved the way for all non-native people living in the modern-day United States. Columbus was quickly perched high on the figures-to-be-iconized list, and, for hundreds of years, he was.

The first recorded instance of a Columbus Day celebration is in October of 1792, when the Society of St. Tammany (also called the Columbian Order) wanted to commemorate the three hundredth anniversary of Columbus's landing in the New World, as he called it. And when President Franklin Delano Roosevelt designated the day to be a national holiday in 1934, Columbus Day became widely celebrated across the country.

All of the events and facts that surround Christopher Columbus are historically murky (like his moral compass). Over the years, historians have discovered a long list of things about the man that had been fictionalized in the name of sounding like a big, bad explorer.

On top of not knowing exactly where (probably Genoa) or when (sometime between 1450 and 1451) Columbus was born, his name might not have even been Christopher Columbus. In Italian, his name would have been Christoforo Colombo, and when he went to Spain it would have been translated as Cristobal Colon. So, there's that.

He claimed he reached the New World in 1492, but he actually landed in the Bahamas around Watling Island, and he thought he had landed in Asia and discovered a new trade route to India. In fact, he never set foot in continental North America, and he certainly didn't discover the New World. Nor was he even the first European explorer to cross the Atlantic; that was Leif Eriksson in 1000 CE.

Hang in there—this *will* eventually involve plants.

What Columbus actually *did* do is painfully clear in historical records (including Columbus's own detailed journals). During his third grand exploration he was arrested by Spanish officials for his gross mismanagement and conduct of one of his colonies—the island he had named " Española," or "Little Spain," now known as Hispaniola, which is split between Haiti and the Dominican Republic.

The island was home to a flourishing indigenous community of Arawak people called the Taíno. After Columbus and his crew landed on the island in 1492, they proceeded to exploit the Taíno people and their island's resources, which resulted in the deaths of hundreds of thousands of people. Prior to Columbus's arrival, the Taíno population was roughly estimated around one million people. Once the Spanish had officially settled on the island in 1507, a more reliable census was taken of the Taíno, whose population had decreased to 60,000. According to local records, by 1531, the population had plummeted to just 600 people. A majority died from European diseases, murder, or enslavement.

So, yeah. Columbus wasn't the most bang-up guy.

And then there was the creation of the Columbian Exchange and triangular trade.

Back in 1453, when Columbus was just a wee lad, the powerhouse city of Constantinople fell to the Ottoman Empire, immediately closing all established trade routes to and from Asia for all of Europe. So, Europeans took to the Atlantic Ocean in hopes of establishing another trade route to Asia—which is where Columbus comes in.

Even though much of what he claimed credit for was fictionalized, Columbus's trips to the Americas kick-started the explorations of those lands by others. This looped the Americas into the European trade route with Africa and Asia, called the Columbian Exchange or triangular trade. Goods, resources, and enslaved people were moved through the trade on a consistent basis, along with disease, violence, and the practice of exploitation.

Plants became a very important resource that were constantly moved across the triangular trade between Europe, the Americas, and Africa.

Plants like tobacco, tomatoes, corn, cocoa, peanuts, and squash moved from the Americas to Europe, and in exchange Europe introduced plants like bananas and coffee from Africa to the Americas. Europe also shipped out manufactured goods like forged metal, woven cloth, and other hard goods to both Africa and the Americas. As European countries continued to colonize Africa, they forced enslaved Africans onto ships and through the Middle Passage of the Atlantic to the Americas to grow cash crops for European profit. As the Europeans spread their grasping fingers across the globe, more and more resources and wealth became available to those in power.

Also passed through the triangular trade were exotic plants from South and Central America that made their way to Europe for the first time to varied success and infinite interest. Plants were pulled up and shipped across the ocean, but not many made it back alive during the long, rough passage across the Atlantic. On top of the plants being subjected to the completely different climate of temperate England, not much was known about caring for tropical plants once they arrived. A small percentage did, however, survive, and they fueled a booming interest in botany and foreign plants during the famed "Age of Discovery."

Enter Sir Hugh Plat

Sir Hugh Plat (sometimes spelled Platt) was a trailblazing agricultural writer at the turn of the seventeenth century. Born in 1552 in London, he started publishing books in 1572 at twenty years old. While not a ton of information is known about his private life, his literary career propelled the trend of keeping houseplants through the centuries all the way to us today.

His father, who was a well-known, successful London brewer, gave Plat the financial support to pursue writing. In 1572 he published *The Floures of Philosophie*, a collection of poems. He followed it up in 1584 with another book of poetry, but then he began to develop quite the obsession with the natural sciences—particularly agriculture and the domestic economy, which he wrote about in 1594 with *The Jewell House of Art and Nature.*

Shortly after, his *Delightes for Ladies, to Adorne Their Persons, Tables, Closets, and Distillatories with Beauties, Banquets, Perfumes, and Waters* was published in 1602. The book was a hit with the housewives of the time. So much so that it was updated in multiple editions over the years. But still, Plat had more to say about gardening and plants.

In 1608 he published *Floraes Paradise*, which was his first major contribution to the field of gardening and agriculture. *Floraes Paradise* is now known as the first gardening manual to have an entire section on indoor plants. *Floraes Paradise* was so popular that there were seven editions of the book published in total, including one under the title *The Garden of Eden* in 1653, published forty-five years after Plat's death by a friend named Charles Bellingham.

Floraes Paradise encouraged people to bring plants into their homes and doled out plenty of advice for lighting, troubleshooting, and general maintenance of houseplants. Plat even explained how to repot, add new soil, and recycle rainwater so that indoor plants would have clean water—quite an innovation for the time!

It's not as if all plants indoors were suddenly turned into hobbies or decoration. Plants in cultivation were still very much utilitarian. From medicines to scented waters and oils, plants ended up being the backbone of the Elizabethan era.

Hygiene in those days was fairly primitive. To our current societal standards, it was pretty bad. Personal hygiene was one thing—people did take baths and manage their teeth (sometimes), but civil hygiene was an entirely different thing.

For example, in London sewage was everywhere because the city's system wasn't built to support the quantity of human waste it received every day. Way back when the Romans ruled London, they had built a functional subterranean sewer system that dumped into the River Thames. However, during the Dark Ages that system was quickly forgotten and fell into disrepair along with everything else the Romans had given society. London turned into a pit of human waste.

In the 1300s there was a law put into place that punished anyone who threw human waste into the river. It was a half-hearted attempt to get people to cart their poop outside of the city limits instead of taking it to the end of the lane and dumping it into the Thames. This was unrealistic, and folks disposed of their waste anywhere and everywhere that was away from their door.

If you lived in even a semipopulated area, it was going to smell. The answer? Waters and oils scented with flowers like roses, lavender, and other herbs. Bowls of scented water sat on dressing tables and trestle tables for frequent handwashing. Even linens were boiled in perfumed water. Herbs were bundled and swept across floors, leaving their scent behind.

Potted herbs and good-smelling plants were frequently set about the home for a little reprieve. Of course, the ultimate trendsetter was the Crown, which inspired common folk to try to make their homes smell as good as the royal palaces. This time period is where we get lavender wands and potpourri from, by the way. Oh, and the cute little fresh posy bouquets everyone wants these days. A few stems of good-smelling flowers go a long way!

The Renaissance

The artistic and scientific rebirth of Europe started slowly brewing around the fourteenth century. During this time, along with advancements in philosophy and literature, an artistic revival was under way, with images that highlighted flowers, fruits, and potted plants in vivacious colors and contrasts. This is where citrus really starts to shine on the European cultivation scene. A guy named John Tradescant the Elder (yes, like *Tradescantia*—it was named after him and his son, John Tradescant the Younger) became a major figure in the plant trade as he traveled the world, even to the Arctic Circle, to send back botanical specimens to England. John Tradescant the Younger traveled to the Americas on several occasions and brought back various exotic plants, including orange and pomegranate trees. Both father and son travelled to three of the four known continents in search of botanical treasures, and each served as the Royal Gardner to the Crown—securing the Tradescant name's place in the history books. Citrus trees of all kinds had been a hit with royalty since the 1200s, but they could be difficult to come by. Royal collectors' plants signified the wealth that it took to acquire and care for such delicate, non-native plants. In the winter they smelled delicious when blooming—yet another way citrus signified wealth by showing that collectors had the means to keep their homes warm enough to keep plants alive during the brutal colder months. The craze for keeping indoor citrus continued right through to modern times. Eight hundred years is quite a long time to remain so popular!

10 Houseplants from Central and South America

Heartleaf Philodendron

Philodendron hederaceum

The Heartleaf Philodendron is one of the most popular houseplants of all time, and it hails from the tropics of South and Central America. It was brought to England's Royal Botanic Gardens in 1793 from the West Indies by Captain William Bligh.

Peace Lily

Spathiphyllum

Peace Lilies are native to southern Mexico, Colombia, and other parts of Central and South America. They get their scientific name from the Greek word "spath," which means spoon, and "phyl," which means leaves—translating to spoon leaves. The most common variety of Peace Lily, the *Spathiphyllum wallisii*—the one with the big, spoon-like white flowers—was brought to Europe from Colombia by Gustav Wallis in 1824.

Tree Philodendron

Philodendron bipinnatifidum

This climbing philodendron is native to the Paranaense forest in Brazil. It produces edible berries and fruits when mature, but rarely indoors. It was named in 1837 by Austrian botanist Heinrich Wilhelm Schott.

Christmas Orchid

Cattleya trianae

This orchid is not only the national flower of Colombia but also one of the largest (and most sought-after) varieties of the cattleya orchid. It is considered one of the most beautiful cattleya varieties in the world.

In 1860, Heinrich Gustav Reichenbach reported that he had discovered it, but in reality, it had been discovered in 1842 by a Belgian explorer named Jean Jules Linden, who failed to collect any specimens. After the discovery was made public, people lost their minds for the flower. Hundreds of thousands of plants were taken from the rain forest and sent to Europe and the United States.

Sensitive Plant

Mimosa pudica

This plant has become famous for its response to physical touch, which causes it to rapidly move its leaves. It's native to South and Central America but is naturalized into the southern United States, Asia, and Africa as a weed. There are records dating back to the seventeenth century that feature this plant in European botanical experiments.

Swiss Cheese Plant

Monstera deliciosa

The *M. deliciosa* is indigenous to the rain forests of southern Mexico and Panama but can be found in many living rooms these days. French botanist Charles Plumier discovered this monstera in 1693.

Rattlesnake Plant

Calathea lancifolia or *Goeppertia insignis*
A native of tropical Brazil, the Rattlesnake Plant thrives in a damp, warm environment. Because it loves humidity so much, it can be difficult to care for indoors in the winter, but that hasn't stopped this plant from ranking on most-popular houseplant lists.

Poinsettia

Euphorbia pulcherrima
Native to southern Mexico, it was first used by native civilizations to dye fabric and control fevers. We now see them most commonly around the holiday season—which is humorous since these are tropical plants that have little to no tolerance for cold weather.

Dr. Joel Roberts Poinsett, a U.S. ambassador to Mexico, introduced the plant to the U.S. after finding (and then naming) it during a nature excursion in 1828.

Bromeliad

There are more than 2,800 species of bromeliad, many of which can be found growing in the wild in Central and South America. Belgian traders began the domestication of the bromeliad when they brought a variety of the plants back to Europe in the 1700s.

Flamingo Lily

Anthurium andraeanum
Also known as the Flamingo Flower, this anthurium has stayed popular for hundreds of years. It is native to Colombia, Ecuador, Venezuelan Antilles, and the Windward Islands. The plant continuously blooms year-round, and the blooms are used frequently in the cut-flower industry.

10 Houseplants That Hail from Africa

The houseplants we adorn our homes with come, naturally, from all over the world. However, it is the continent of Africa that we have to thank for many of the most popular houseplants on the market—and that deserves to be celebrated.

Snake Plant

Dracaena trifasciata
Also known as Mother-in-Law's Tongue and sansevieria, the *Dracaena trifasciata* is native to western Africa, from Nigeria to the Congo.

Spider Plant

Chlorophytum comosum
This common houseplant is native to the tropics of western and southern Africa but can also be found naturalized in western Australia.

ZZ Plant

Zamioculcas zamiifolia
This novice-proof houseplant comes from the drier grasslands and forests of eastern Africa.

Aloe Vera

Aloe barbadensis miller
Originally, you'd be able to find this plant growing in northern Africa, southern Europe, and the Canary Islands. However, now this useful plant has been naturalized across the globe.

Zebra Plant

Haworthiopsis fasciata
This succulent is native to the Eastern Cape of South Africa.

African Violet

Saintpaulia spp.
African violets, the darling of the windowsill, are indigenous to the forests of Tanzania and southern Kenya.

Fiddle-Leaf Fig

Ficus lyrata
The *F. lyrata* is native to the lowland rain forests of western Africa.

Jade Plant

Crassula ovata
The Jade Plant is thought by some to bring good luck. As it grows and ages, it takes the shape of a small tree. It's native to South Africa.

Bird of Paradise

Strelitzia nicolai

This glamorous, must-have houseplant staple is native to coastal southern Africa. It produces the popular Bird of Paradise flower that is used by tropical florists all over the world.

String of Pearls

Senecio rowleyanus

Everyone loves this cute little succulent, which is indigenous to the drier areas of the southwestern regions of Africa.

CHAPTER 6

King Louis XIV and His Citrus Obsession

EARLY MODERN FRANCE (1643–1715)

King Louis XIV had such a significant impact on the indoor cultivation of plants that he needed his very own chapter in this book. Louis ascended the throne at age fourteen and went on to build one of the most exclusive, extravagant palaces of all time: Versailles. Over his seventy-two-year reign, he collected more than three thousand citrus plants for his orangery. His obsession was directly responsible for the popularity of indoor plants skyrocketing across Europe. More gardening books were published, a variety of greenhouses were built, and—surprise! A thriving rental market for plants popped up for people who wanted to mimic the plant-happy lifestyle of the rich. Things got even crazier once "tulipomania" descended on Western Europe.

After this royal tour, you'll learn how to create your own lemon arbor indoors, why you should consider renting your houseplants, and information about a few famous Kew plants that you can keep in your own home.

The Orangerie of Versailles

King Louis XIV was an extravagant monarch. He was a young, reckless king who liked to spend his country's money on decadence. In the late 1650s, frightened of an impending civil war, he fled the city of Paris and took refuge at the royal hunting lodge in Versailles.

Once there, he decided that a rustic hunting lodge was no place for a bougie boy-king and set about making some changes. From 1661 to 1682, Louis XIV did a little remodel on the place, transforming it into the grand Palace of Versailles. He effectively moved the entirety of his court from Paris to the new palace and transformed Versailles into the European epicenter of political power and luxury.

But that still wasn't enough for our boy-king. Louis also wanted to create one of the most exclusive gardens in all of Europe, and so was born the Orangerie of Versailles, a completely enclosed building dedicated to cultivating the extensive royal collection of citrus trees. The building itself is an architectural masterpiece. For the warmer months a parterre, or level garden space, was built just outside the orangery for the citrus trees to take in the sun.

After the completion of the new royal palace, Louis XIV tapped architect Jules Hardouin-Mansart to expand the existing orangery. It took Jules two years to double the size of the space to an expansive 492 feet with forty-two-foot-high ceilings. Jules also followed the teachings of expert gardener Jean-Baptiste de La Quintinie, who studied how to keep delicate, exotic flora from getting too cold without wasting resources on heating. Doubled windows and sixteen-foot-thick walls prevented the temperature in the room from dipping below 40 degrees Fahrenheit.

Louis XIV took all of the citrus trees from his other palaces and brought them to Versailles. He also began a large acquisition of even more citrus from all over Europe, eventually bringing his collection to more than three thousand specimens. The trees were planted in boxes made of cast iron and oak, created by famed landscape gardener André Le Nôtre exclusively for Versailles.

Versions of these boxes are still used today at Versailles. If you visit the orangery today, you'll notice that the citrus trees bloom throughout the year. For hundreds of years, the gardeners of Versailles have used special techniques that involve moderating water and nutrients alongside sophisticated pruning methods in order to ensure the yearlong blooms. After all, what the king wants—he gets.

Tulipomania

During the 1600s all of Europe collectively lost its mind over tulips. A Dutch man named Carolus Clusius, who was the head botanist of Western Europe's first botanic garden, came into some very pretty, very rare tulip bulbs from central Asia. He introduced them to Holland and unknowingly set the stage for a continent-wide craze.

The tulip bulbs that Clusius had in his possession at the botanic garden slowly started to make their way to the public, one leaked bulb at a time. Limited supply and high demand launched tulip bulbs into the rare plant trade. Flowering bulbs in general were hot commodities due to how easily they bloomed indoors. These bulbs could be brought inside the home to flower during the winter months, and then quickly and cleanly removed once they were spent. But there weren't enough of these tulip bulbs to go around. Tulip prices rose, and all through the early 1600s the prices kept rising. Botanists created hybrids, but instead of quelling the demand, the new blooms were even more sought after.

Wealthy collectors were willing to pay any price for the rarest, most beautiful tulip bulb. It was recorded in 1624 that one variety sold at $1,500 per bulb, which is roughly $50,000 today. A short time after, that audacious sale was topped by one bulb going for $2,250 (more than $100,000 today), though that one came with a few bonus items: a horse and a carriage.

As with any trend, tulipomania would not live forever. Money was spent up, scammers infiltrated the market, and bulb prices plummeted to a normal rate. But even though the market stabilized, the public continued to invest quite a bit of money and time in tulips and flowering bulbs in general. Later, during the eighteenth century, the bulb market blossomed again as the market for decorative plant containers heated up. Cachepots and other planters adorned mantles and shelves and cabinets all over the world, providing conditions inside that allowed bulbs to bloom. And Holland is still the top-producing exporter of tulip bulbs in the entire world—nine billion tulip bulbs are produced there every year.

Hothouses and Hotheaded Europeans

Throughout the seventeenth century, hothouses had been built all over Europe as additions to wealthy manors and royal palaces, a trend that continued into the 1700s. By the middle of the eighteenth century, it had become relatively easy to purchase and care for plants meant to be grown indoors. These hothouses kept finicky, exotic plants thriving in all seasons and regions. Of course, Europeans thought they were revolutionary by creating heated greenhouses, but the first heated greenhouse was actually constructed during the Joseon dynasty in Korea back in the 1450s. It used a subfloor heating system that also helped keep the hothouse humid for prime vegetable growth and production. These greenhouses were also used to protect precious mandarin trees during cold snaps.

European heated greenhouses were commonly called "stoves," after the Old English word "stofa," which meant an enclosed space, like a small room. The old phrase "stoved in" meant something akin to being cooped up, and this usage of "stove" for hothouse or heated greenhouse was in place well into the nineteenth century. Words are tricky, and the language of botanical literature from this era is no exception. Sometimes certain words like "stove" were used to refer to slightly different types of greenhouses. But whatever they were called, the "stove" was the designated room where many high-profile collectors kept their most expensive and rare tropical specimens.

These early European hothouses were a huge pain. England's first heated greenhouse was completed in 1681 at the Chelsea Physic Garden in London, where it quickly became apparent that these structures were very expensive to build and maintain. Many plants bit the dust during this lengthy era of experimentation.

As mechanics and materials improved, heated greenhouses became more common around the sixteenth century. Wealthy Europeans routinely sponsored plant collectors to go out on international expeditions and bring back the rarest, most interesting plants they could find. Once the plants arrived to the collector, no expense was too great to keep their treasures alive. Simulating a tropical environment cost an absolute fortune, and then there was the added cost of hiring people to care for those plants. Luckily, folks who could afford these heated greenhouses weren't hard up for cash.

The 1700s was also a great time for folks who didn't want to—or couldn't—hire plant hunters to go chasing the rarest bounty. Cultivars became available through nurseries. Nurserymen hired their own plant hunters and acquired and cultivated plants for the retail market. It was also possible to get quality plants at the popular Convent Garden, London's daily marketplace. Retail greenhouses also began offering services that were akin to modern-day plant rentals and plant sitting. No one wanted to be caught hosting an event without beautiful indoor plants.

How to Force Bulbs to Bloom Indoors

"Forcing" in botany is the simple process of making a plant flower in an artificial environment. Outdoor-growing bulbs are planted in the fall so they can overwinter and generate energy for spring blooms, but you can bypass months of waiting by forcing bulbs to bloom indoors within a matter of weeks. It is an easy process that will have you thinking that you've played a fast one on Mother Nature.

There are many different types of bulbs that you can force indoors, depending on your personal preferences. Commonly forced bulbs include crocus, paperwhite, amaryllis, daffodil, hyacinth, grape hyacinth, iris, and snowdrop. Some blooms will have a strong scent, while others will barely have one at all. It's best to do your research beforehand if you have a sensitivity to some smells. For example, paperwhites have a very strong scent that is off-putting to many people.

One of the hardest parts of forcing bulbs is finding where to source the actual bulbs. If you order online from an unreliable source, you could end up with product that has been temperature damaged due to improper transport or packaging. If you do decide to source your bulbs online, be sure to research multiple outlets and read reviews. Also, keep an eye out for "prechilled" bulbs; they'll save you even more time, as you won't have to wait as long for blooms. Bulbs need a cooling period—which mimics winter—in order to get ready to grow.

Your best bet is to source from local plant nurseries. Most garden shops will have a wide selection of prechilled bulbs that are ready to force. You'll even be able to find preplanted bulbs that are already growing in beautiful arrangements, just waiting for you to take home.

If you're growing amaryllis or paperwhites, you won't have to worry about chilling them, as they're naturally tropical plants and do not need a cold snap. You can plant those and see blooms in three to eight weeks (amaryllis will take the most time to bloom). Most other bulbs will need to be prechilled, or you can chill them yourself in the vegetable drawer of your refrigerator or an unheated part of your home (like the basement or garage). Keep them away from moisture unless you're planting them in soil, which we will cover later!

The chill time for some common bulbs is:

Tulip: 10–15 weeks; blooms 2–3 weeks after planting
> Native Habitat: *There are more than 100 species, but most are native to Asia and the Mediterranean.*

Snowdrop: 15 weeks; blooms 2 weeks after planting
> Native Habitat: *Europe and the Middle East*

Iris: 13–15 weeks; blooms 2–3 weeks after planting
> Native Habitat: *Europe and Asia*

Crocus: 8–15 weeks; blooms 2–3 weeks after planting
> Native Habitat: *Europe, the Middle East, and China*

Hyacinth: 12–15 weeks; blooms 2–3 weeks after planting
> Native Habitat: *The Mediterranean and the Middle East*

Grape Hyacinth: 8–14 weeks; blooms 2–3 weeks after planting
> Native Habitat: *Southeastern Europe*

Daffodil: 2–3 weeks; blooms 2–3 weeks after planting
Native Habitat: *Northern Europe*

For January blooms, chill in September. For February blooms, chill in October. For March blooms, chill in November. For April blooms, chill in December, and so on.

If you're looking for a mess-free way to force bulbs, you'll want to use a container and water. All you'll need is a prechilled bulb, pebbles, and a vessel.

1. Pick your container. You can use a vase or favorite vintage container like a teapot, shallow bowl, or wide-mouthed vase. Many people favor a special type of vase called a forcing vase, which is purpose-built for forcing bulbs. These take the guesswork out of the process, and you'll be able to clearly see if your bulb is sitting in the water (something that can cause the bulb to rot). If you choose to use a forcing vase, skip to step 4. If you're using a regular vase or other type of vessel, read on.

2. Layer a few inches of pebbles in the bottom of your vessel.

3. Nestle your prechilled bulbs, tip up, among the pebbles. Press the bulbs down gently so that they are secure.

4. Pour water into the container until the water level is just below the bottom of the bulbs. Whatever you do, don't let the water reach the bulbs. If your bulbs sit in water, they will rot before they get a chance to bloom. The idea is for the roots to grow down to the water.

5. Place your vessel away from direct sunlight. Leave it there until the bulbs begin to root. If you're using an opaque container, gently pull on the bulb to see if it gives any resistance (if it's rooting, it will). At this point you should be at the two-to-three-week mark. Bulbs like tulips and amaryllis will take a little longer. During this time add water when the level is at less than one inch in the vessel.

6. Once your bulbs have rooted, you can move the vessel to a bright, sunny spot in your home. Still keep an eye on the water level; they will be taking in more water at this time. Once you begin to see the stem shoot up, it won't be long (a week or two) until the bulb blooms.

If the latter isn't up your alley, try forcing bulbs in soil. This method is a little more involved than forcing bulbs in just water. You'll need a container, bulbs, potting mix, and access to a place to chill the bulbs (unless you're using prechilled bulbs or planting amaryllis or paperwhites).

1. Choose a container for your bulbs.

2. Fill the container with damp potting mix until it is three-quarters full.

3. Place the bulbs pointy end up on the surface of the soil. Group the bulbs close together so they are more cloistered.

4. Cover the bulbs until only the points are sticking out of the surface of the soil.

5. If you aren't chilling your bulbs, skip this step. If you are: Place your bulbs in a cool, dark place such as a basement, unheated porch, or garage. Chill them for the required amount of time. Keep the soil lightly damp during chilling.

6. After the required amount of time has passed, move your bulbs into your home, out of direct sunlight. If you've just planted prechilled bulbs or bulbs that don't require a chilling period, move them to a place that is out of the direct sunlight. Leave them there until the bulbs begin to take root, which should take two to three weeks after chilling. You can check by gently tugging on each bulb to see if it gives resistance. Only water when the potting mix is dry to the touch. Overwatering will encourage rot.

7. Once your bulbs have rooted, move the container to a sunny spot in your home. Water when the soil becomes dry to the touch. Once the stems begin to emerge from the soil, you should see blooms in two to three weeks.

So, what do you do after you've coaxed your bulbs into blooming? Each type of bulb has a different bloom time, which is also dependent on the type of care they receive. You can stretch your bloom life up to roughly twenty days if you give it a solid effort. Some tips:

- After your bulbs have begun to flower, move the container out of the direct sun to a cooler place in your home. Direct sun will cause the blooms to decay at a more rapid pace.
- Don't leave your blooms near any type of heating element, including radiators, fireplaces, space heaters, and air vents. It's also a good rule of thumb to keep bulbs away from extreme temperature changes, so avoid placing them near doors that open to the outside.
- Don't be afraid to trim off dying blooms. Dead blooms pressing against newer ones will decrease bloom time.
- Only water your bulbs when the soil is dry to the touch. Overwatering will promote bulb rot, which is something you cannot see until it's too late.

You might find that some of your bulbs have bloomed, while others haven't even sprouted. If this happens, something probably happened to the underperforming bulbs before they got to you. They were likely either harvested or stored incorrectly or have some kind of rot.

After all the blooms are spent, you might find yourself struggling with throwing them in the trash. Can you keep and reuse the bulbs next year? This really varies from person to person. Some people like the process of saving their bulbs and putting them into dormancy in order to start the process all over again the following year. However, it's worth noting that this is a complicated process, and bulbs might not perform as well the second time around. They're also a low-cost investment, so feel free to compost spent bulbs and buy fresh ones for your next growing season.

YOUR LEAFY LEGACY:
Grow Your Own Indoor Lemon Tree

Walk into a retail nursery at any time of year and you're going to stumble upon a citrus tree ready to bear fruit for its new family. More than likely that beauty is the ever-popular lemon tree. There's no denying the appeal of a potted lemon tree, and keeping citrus trees indoors is far from a new fad. For hundreds of years, lemon trees have been making waves in gardens and homes across the world. Their fragrant blooms and delicious fruits keep them in high demand, whether you have a chateau in the French countryside or a studio apartment in Brooklyn.

It's easy to fall in love with lemon trees, and easy to care for them too. You won't need your own personal gardener to maintain your private citrus grove. Caring for these plants is pretty easy—if you can follow a few rules.

Find the Right Lemon Tree to Grow Indoors

Do a little digging, and you'll find that there are many different lemon trees to choose from that vary in size, stature, and fruit. A few varieties are better suited for being grown in a container.

Many local nurseries offer terrific options when it comes to citrus. If you're a beginner or worried about keeping a full-size tree, look for a dwarf variety that is easier to care for. The Lisbon, dwarf Ponderosa, and Meyer are "improved" dwarf varieties that are better suited for container growing than larger cultivars. Another thing to keep in mind: Most lemon trees do not bear fruit until they are three to four years old. Do yourself a favor and buy a more mature tree, especially if you're looking to have fruit within the first year of ownership.

Pot in Terra-Cotta

Many growers choose to grow their lemon trees in terra-cotta pots because they help keep the soil from becoming oversaturated with water. But there isn't anything wrong with planting your tree in a plastic or glazed pot as long as there are drainage holes. Lemon trees do not like sitting in water.

Also, as a standard rule of thumb, the container needs to be at least two inches larger than the root ball of the plant. This helps promote growth and keeps your plant healthy.

Choose the Right Soil

You'll be able to find citrus potting mix at any local nursery or online. The soil needs to be a compound that will dry out easily. If you need to make your own mix, combine regular potting mix with equal parts sand for the same feel. A citrus mix will help prevent overwatering and will mimic your tree's ideal natural environment.

Shine the Light

This is where it can get tricky while caring for lemon trees. All citrus plants need a ton of bright light in order to thrive indoors—more than ten hours per day. The best place for an indoor lemon tree would be in a south-facing window. Without enough light the plant will not produce flowers, and therefore will not produce fruit. If you're worried about your light situation, try supplementing with a grow light.

Keep Your Tree Toasty

Temperature is particularly important when growing lemon trees indoors. These plants do not like cold temperatures, nor do they like radical temperature change. This means that you need to keep them away from forced-air vents, doors that open outside, radiators, drafty windows, and fireplaces. Lemon trees thrive at steady temperatures between 50 and 80 degrees Fahrenheit.

Don't Forget to Water!

Even though lemon trees are native to the Mediterranean and thrive in arid environments, it is important to water your tree regularly. When the soil is dry one to two inches deep (roughly two knuckles into the soil), pour water into the pot until it runs out the drainage holes and into the tray. Let your lemon tree dry between each watering. This means that your watering schedule will be different in the summer than it will be in the winter. You might end up watering your tree every week in the summer but only every two or three weeks in the winter.

For an added boost, mist the leaves a few times a week and fertilize with a high-nitrogen product made for citrus trees. Be sure to read the instructions. Overfertilizing your tree can give it chemical burn.

Prepare for Pests

Keep on the lookout for regular houseplant pests like aphids and spider mites. Lemon tree leaves are especially yummy, which makes these plants extremely vulnerable to pests. If your plant gets stressed from overwatering or under-watering, insufficient light, or extreme temperature change, it will become more susceptible to unwanted guests.

Bringing Your Citrus Plants to Fruition

Sometimes a lemon tree kept indoors will figure out how to pollinate itself without help, but most of the time they will need your assistance. All you need is a cotton swab or small paintbrush. The only tricky part is figuring out which part of the flower is male and which part is female. The male parts, called anthers, will be protruding from the bloom and will be covered in pollen. Coat your swab or brush with the pollen.

Find the female part of the flower, called the stigma, which is in the middle of the bloom and will be sticky. Coat as much of the stigma as possible with the pollen you've collected. You'll know if you were successful when the bloom begins to grow a small fruit.

YOUR LEAFY LEGACY:
Rent Your Plants!

"Fake it 'til you make it" has been a thing for forever. In the 1700s if you didn't have plants in your home, you didn't belong in the upper social echelons, so many people turned to getting plants on loan from local greenhouses and nurserymen for events or as temporary decor for the cooler months when greenery indoors was a welcome, posh respite from the winter.

While houseplants aren't quite the status symbol they used to be (I mean, I guess it depends on who you're talking to), renting plants for your office or for events is still completely acceptable.

If you're not interested in having a collection but *need* the lush look of plants for a period of time, rental is the way to go. Looking to refresh your professional space or restaurant? Rent some plants. Need a ton of plants for a wedding? Rent them. Having a large get-together like a reunion, bar mitzvah, or Victorian-themed dinner party? Rent some plants!

There are some built-in bonuses if you do:

Expertise

When renting plants, there's a solid chance that you'll be getting some A-class consulting on the product that you need. People in the plant business love to help clients pick the right plants and correct all-too-common misinformation. That's what we live for! Let the nice plant people help you.

Before you meet, make a list of what you might be looking for and bring it with you. If you don't know what the plants are called that you have in mind, bring some pictures. Putting your thoughts together ahead of time will give you an extra boost of confidence when you head into the consultation.

They Come Potted

If you're familiar with the plant trends, you know that pottery and containers are a big part of the overall look of houseplants. If you outright purchase plants from a shop, they usually come in a plastic grower's pot instead of pretty pottery. But rental plants come in nice, aesthetically pleasing pots, if that floats your boat. You won't have to worry about the extra expense or time spent picking out pots.

Fancy Plants

In a world obsessed with appearances, it's easy to get caught in that mindset even in plant parenthood. And even if it's what's on the inside that counts, we all want plants that look good, especially if they're decor for a special event. When you rent plants, you can rest assured that you'll have your pick of the best-looking plants around. Brokers and rental companies aren't going to show up with brown, crispy product. It's their business, and if they're any good at what they do, they'll follow through for their clients.

You Don't Have to Transport Them

If you live in an urban area or simply don't have the desire to transport plants to your home, office, or event, plant rental is a great option for you. Even plant professionals find transporting plants challenging. Leave it to the professionals! All you have to do is pick out the plants, put a deposit down, and hand over the information for the time and address for the delivery. It's as easy as that.

Ultimately Someone Else's Problem

The best part of the whole shebang is that you won't be on the hook for caring for these plants. For short-term rentals, the company will come and pick them up before they need to be watered, or before they end up with environmental damage. For long-term rentals, companies usually set up a weekly or biweekly schedule where some lovely human will come water and provide general care for the plants. All you have to do is sit back and admire the beauty.

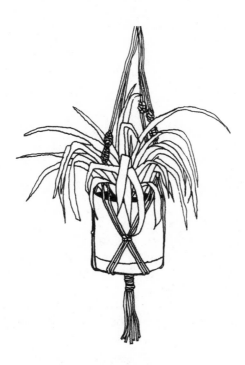

CHAPTER 7

A Bougie Victorian Invents the Terrarium

THE NINETEENTH CENTURY (1800–1899)

The European bourgeoisie became powerful tastemakers during the nineteenth century. No surprises there—bougie is bougie. But suddenly houseplants were making frequent appearances in a majority of homes. There were better systems for indoor heating (and greenhouses!), so plants didn't freeze to death. They did, however, struggle to thrive with all of that air pollution from industrialization. Then an amateur plant enthusiast named Nathaniel Bagshaw Ward accidentally invented the terrarium in 1829. Many plants were purchased, books were written, and terrariums were built. The Victorian passion for terrariums kick-started a massive trend that trickled across commercial and scientific industries and is still popular today.

Settle in, loosen your corset strings, and let's jump into the Victorian era.

Middle-Class Victory for Plants: The Industrial Revolution

The nineteenth century was revolutionary, and not just in the plant world. For the first time in European history, there existed a societal upper-middle class. The emergence of the bourgeoisie—the monied but not aristocratic class that emerged from the Industrial Revolution—coincided with the rising emphasis on property. Owning fancy things was very, very important.

Comfortable living had become a little more affordable. Heating systems for homes became cleaner and more efficient with the invention of steam boilers. Clean water was easier to access (mostly—don't ask the Brontës about this), and later in the century, indoor plumbing became available for those who could or wanted to pay for it.

Needless to say, it was still extremely rough going for the lower classes. These technological advancements extended lifespans and allowed people to have larger families and a better chance at employment, but pay was frequently below the living wage, and many families had no choice but to send their children into the workforce. It is thought that at times during the nineteenth century up to 50 percent of the workforce in London were children under the age of eighteen. Tenements were overcrowded, and the streets were flooded with human waste, all while the middle and upper classes were enjoying unprecedented comfort and ease.

All of these luxuries that the upper classes could afford were, however, beneficial to any plant in cultivation. Thinner and better-quality glass for greenhouses became available around the middle of the century across Europe, and the steam boilers that were pumping out cleaner and more efficient heat also produced humid air, which tropical plants love. Clean water also helped plants thrive longer in cultivation.

If plants could thrive in your parlor year-round, that meant you had access to clean water and heat—if you cultivated plants, it meant you were a person of certain means.

Not everyone had those means, but many people wanted to come off like they did. Enter the hardy houseplants: the plants that can withstand a fair amount of neglect, minimal watering, and mediocre light. The popularity of these types of plants is a trend that started in the middle of the nineteenth century, and we have the Victorians to thank for it.

If you look at any Victorian-era portrait or family photo, you'll notice that there are plants in just about every image. Odds are some of those plants are either Kentia Palms or aspidistras. Even George Orwell took a jab at this status-obsessed society when he published *Keep the Aspidistra Flying* in 1936.

These plants, which are still very popular and easy to find today, are extremely resilient. Kentia Palms *(Howea forsteriana)* were at the top of the popularity list for middle-class Victorians. Native to Australia, these plants made their way across Europe via esteemed collectors and plant hunters, and then trickled down into the homes of more common men. The Kentia's leaf structure and impressive height made it a great floor plant for grand parlors and entryways. These palms were also a popular choice in hotels and shops of the time. They have the ability to thrive in low humidity, low light, and cooler temperatures where other species of palms would wither and die off. And, along with Lily of the Valley and pelargonium, the Kentia Palm was a particular favorite of the ultimate Victorian tastemaker, Queen Victoria herself.

The aspidistra is native to Japan, and even though it's relatively slow growing compared with the Kentia Palm, it is almost indestructible—thus its nickname, the "cast iron plant." It pretty much survived everything the Victorians could throw at it, be it neglect or heavy air pollution. Both the Kentia Palm and the aspidistra became a hallmark of middle-class luxury, and they were everywhere—pretty much the only game in town—that is, until 1829.

The Accidental Invention

The modern terrarium is one of the most versatile decorative plant accessories available to us in the twenty-first century. There are open terrariums (great for desert plants) and traditional closed terrariums (for your tropicals) available in all shapes and sizes. You can find terrariums that hang delicately from the ceiling, fixtures that take up copious amounts of real estate on coffee tables, and glass vessels that will stand tall on your bookshelves. From custom pieces worthy of being called "furniture," to at-home DIY plant bottles, terrarium gardening is still a happening scene in the plant world. These containers look great in the home and are relatively easy to care for as long as they're looked after correctly. You can find terrariums at every plant store, home goods shop, and craft retailer—and if you can't find what you want there, online selections are seemingly infinite.

So, how exactly did this variety of container gardening become so popular? Naturally, we can blame the Victorians, and there is a rich history packed between those glass panels. The Victorian period is named for the reign of Queen Victoria, from 1837 through 1901, but the zeitgeist of England started changing during the Georgian years in the late 1820s. The Victorians were obsessed with all kinds of newfangled notions, from social-class mobility to dabbling in the occult to new literary forms. Plants were as popular in Victorian literature as they were in their parlors. Oscar Wilde was known to toss dozens of plant references in his books, and Robert Louis Stevensen wrote *A Child's Garden of Verses*, along with a bunch of other swoon-worthy garden-themed poetry.

The Victorians really, really loved their plants. Innovations in indoor heating and architecture allowed for bigger windows and higher ceilings, which created the perfect atmosphere for bringing plants indoors. Similar advancements allowed homes to be lit with lamps that were fueled by gas. Gone were the days of squinting by candlelight or oil lamps—at least for the certain classes. It was a great expense to have gas lighting installed and maintained, so it was only available to the upper echelon.

These advancements, however, did not come without downsides. The gas fixtures emitted so many noxious chemicals that it became almost impossible to keep delicate houseplants like ferns and violets alive in gaslit houses. All of the innovations that kept botanical specimens alive inside were powerless against the fumes. With the exception of a few true hardy plants like Kentia Palms and aspidistras, very little could thrive indoors during this time. And, honestly, if you lived in an urban center, cultivating a garden outside wasn't an easy task either. The outdoor air quality was so poor that many garden plants withered and died not long after emerging from the earth.

Enter Nathaniel Bagshaw Ward. In 1829, Ward was just a plant lover trying to get a few plants to survive indoors. As a child he developed a great fondness for botany and tried many times in vain to get different fern varieties to grow along the garden wall of his family's home in London. As an adult, he was a doctor by trade but kept his deep love for plants of all kinds, which he studied obsessively as a hobby. Although he had rotten luck keeping his plants alive, he did have marginal success in hatching moths, butterflies, and other fauna.

One day, in 1829, Ward examined a bottle in which he had placed a chrysalis for a sphinx moth. Among the damp soil that lined the bottom was a rogue fern spore that had sprouted, seemingly overnight, in the sealed bottle. Fascinated, Ward spent hours observing the condensation in the bottle—how the moisture rose from the damp soil to the top of the bottle, and then rolled back down the curve of the glass.

He realized that this process kept the soil continuously damp and the humidity level consistently high. He had created a miniature water cycle inside of the bottle: the perfect environment for delicate, exotic plants to thrive within.

From that bottle, Ward's innovation, which he named the Wardian case—what we now know as the terrarium—was born.

At the time, large greenhouse additions could be added to a home or built as standalone structures for botanists and plant collectors, but nothing had ever been designed for indoor plant cultivation on a smaller, mobile scale. Ward built his cases to the size of a side table or small writing desk. He used glazed windowpanes that sealed the cases, so that the final product was completely enclosed—safe from any pollution. This allowed condensation to form and release freely within the case, creating an independent ecosystem. The design also allowed for limited human care. Plants that were placed within rarely—if ever—needed to be watered, especially if the seal was never broken.

Ward kept that first bottle for four years and never opened it. The plants lived until he accidentally left it on an open windowsill and the cap rusted through, allowing contaminated rainwater to enter the vessel. London's Great Exhibition of 1851 featured a Wardian case with a plant that had allegedly not been watered in more than eighteen years, which was quite the sensation.

Throughout the rest of the nineteenth century, the Wardian case was used to transport botanical specimens that had been found in the British colonies and beyond. Many Victorian botanists revered Ward as a genius for his invention and used the cases on expeditions across the globe. Where before only a very small percentage of collected plants would survive the journey back to England, the Wardian case ensured a much higher survival rate, sometimes up to 100 percent.

As commercial use expanded, Wardian cases became a staple in upper-class homes all across Western Europe and the United States. Their designs became more intricate, with large, ornate bases and miniature glass turrets—gorgeous pieces of utilitarian furniture. Horticultural literature featured case designs of all kinds. Popular books like multiple editions of Shirley Hibberd's *Rustic Adornments for Homes of Taste* and monthly women's magazines like *Peterson's* touted Wardian cases as the must-have parlor decoration.

Like much of the bounty of the British Empire, many of the plants transported in Wardian cases were stolen from their native habitats in the name of science. Many of those smuggled plants ended up in conservatories and trickled down to the common houseplants we have today.

As for Nathaniel Bagshaw Ward, he had his fifteen minutes of fame—but eventually lost face with professional botanists after he claimed to have created the largest Wardian case in the world, which ended up being an unsealed glass conservatory masquerading as a giant terrarium. Gossip spread that he was only after fame and was desperate to be known as "a second Newton." Whether that was true or not, Ward slowly lost clout and credibility within the botanical community and died almost penniless. He is buried in an unmarked grave in West Norwood Cemetery in London.

The Heated Greenhouse Gets an Upgrade

If you're thinking of a Victorian greenhouse, you're likely thinking of a structure built in a very particular style. The name evokes images of grandiose buildings made of glass and iron and brimming with wild, vining plants. In truth, that's not far off from what the Victorians had in mind when they modified the hothouse into what we now know as the modern-day greenhouse. The nineteenth century saw the construction of some of the largest, most glorious greenhouses and conservatories ever built.

The trendiness and availability (or sometimes even the scarcity) of "exotic" plants during this time drove the need for more glass houses to put them in. Where else were rich people going to keep their fancy plants? From the outset, these glass beauties were only attainable by the upper classes. These buildings weren't cheap—particularly after the introduction of the 1746 British glass tax by King George II. The glass tax was determined by weight, which if you were building a greenhouse added up quickly; the recommended glass weight was twenty-one ounces to the square foot.

The tax wasn't abolished until 1846, but greenhouses remained a luxury because of the standing window tax (such creativity!). That one wasn't repealed until the 1850s.

Victorian Glasshouse 101

What we now think of as a typical greenhouse didn't exist in the nineteenth century. There were a few different types of plant houses at the time, with some similarities and lots of differences. They were:

1. The Greenhouse

The name "greenhouse" referred to a building that housed temperate plants. It was a moderate-size building that was kept between 40 and 70 degrees Fahrenheit—never too hot and never too cold. Greenhouses were used to keep plants that grow quickly and flower in a warm, moist atmosphere and that could tolerate moderately fluctuating temperatures. These plants were frequently taken into the home for decor. Once these plants started to decline or die, they were either tossed into the compost pile or taken back to the greenhouse to reestablish a healthy growing pattern. Herbaceous plants like daylilies, geraniums, pelargoniums, and so forth were also grown in greenhouses but rarely kept longer than a growing season. Many growers and collectors grew new stock each season and kept permanent shelf space reserved for "rarer" plants.

2. The Conservatory

The conservatory was a structure that was only affordable to the ultra-elite. It was a larger, loftier glass building that was showier than the standard greenhouse. Still, it also housed temperate plants and was kept at moderate temperatures. Conservatories were primarily filled with fancy plant displays. Plants were usually set up tall to short, in groupings. This created the effect of a building packed with plants. The more plants you had, the higher your social status. The types of plants housed in conservatories were similar to those grown in the greenhouses; there were just more of them.

3. The Orchid House

Also known as a "hothouse" or a "stove," this was where folks kept their high-dollar, tropical, imported plants. Temperatures were kept between 70 and 90 degrees Fahrenheit—the perfect environment for orchids, aroids, and ferns. A hothouse kept on the drier side was perfect for succulents and cacti and would be called a "cacti house."

These different types of glass houses were all constructed in a similar fashion. There were many factors to be considered, like how the house should be placed in relation to the home and how the owner was going to use it. It was widely understood that iron construction was the only way to build. Wood was understood to be an extremely subpar material, along with any kind of glass that wasn't English.

Once the construction was sorted, you had to know how you were going to heat the thing to keep plants alive and thriving. Oddly enough, the bigger the glass house, the easier it was to heat and regulate. The environment in smaller glass houses fluctuated too easily—a small change like a door left open could mean a big change for your delicate plants.

At the cusp of the Industrial Revolution, there were multiple options to choose from when it came to heating. There was the traditional flue system that relied on a brick flue and furnace. This was the simplest method, and one that relied solely on wood for fuel. This was also the method that most people would have been familiar with when it came to heating.

Another option was the boiler, which was a new, flashy technology that heated greenhouses with coal or wood. Then came hot-water boilers. All these new options made it slightly overwhelming to choose the best one for the individual's needs, and the learning curve was quite steep. A lot of pricey plants met their end as plant keepers figured out their heating systems.

Bougie Glasshouses

During the Victorian era, a whole bunch of bougie, high-dollar conservatories were built in England. The Great Conservatory at Chatsworth House was completed in 1840 by architect Joseph Paxton. At the time it was the largest glass building in England, only to be outdone by Paxton's own Crystal Palace in 1851.

Kew Royal Botanic Gardens is known globally for having one of the largest and most diverse botanical collections in the world. Created in 1840, it is now one of the most important institutions for botanical research. On site, there are multiple greenhouses and conservatories. The Nash Conservatory was moved to the Kew site in 1836 after originally being constructed at Buckingham Palace by King William IV. The Palm House was built between 1844 and 1848, and the Waterlily House was constructed in 1849. The Temperate House, the Orangery, and the bonsai house also sit on the property.

The Crystal Palace was built in 1851 for the Great Exhibition in Hyde Park, London. From May to October, the Crystal Palace showcased how modern architecture was progressing alongside the advancements of the Industrial Revolution. Designed by Paxton, it was three times larger than St. Paul's Cathedral—one of the biggest structures in London at that time.

The Victorian Potting Bench

Even the most amateur plant collector's greenhouse had a similar operating system to the fanciest conservatories and glass houses. Without an established routine, all cultivated indoor plants would (and will) fail to thrive. And the cultivator needs certain skills and tools to put a successful routine into place.

Keeping a plant collection in cultivation in a glass house meant that each plant needed to be grown in its own pot. And if you're growing plants in pots, you're going to need a potting shed or potting section in your greenhouse. The Victorians did not slack on the potting mix they used for their plants. Even amateur gardeners knew that certain plants liked certain mixes of soil. A typical potting soil mix included some version of the following: loam, peat, sand, leaf mold, pot shards, old manure, and old mortar/plaster. This combination of materials ensured a light, airy potting mix, perfect for younger plants and plants with more delicate root systems.

Potting and repotting plants was a test of dexterity. It was a challenge to know when to repot, especially during an era when botanical knowledge was less advanced than it is now. Common sense and your intuition were often all you had to aid you with the troubleshooting process. At that time, repotting was called "shifting," as in shifting a plant from one pot to another.

Most plants in greenhouses were raised from cuttings, so it was important to baby them into maturity. Only then would you be able to keep them thriving for the entire season.

Insects and Disease

Once you figured out the heating and care and repotting trial and error that is plant collection, you'd have to deal with pests.

Greenflies, red spider mites—also called red ants—scale, and mildew were rampant in glass houses. Fortunately for the Victorians, most of these pests could be cleared up with fresh air, water, and more or less light exposure. Supplement those measures with era-appropriate remedies like tobacco powder, sulfur, soot, or lime, and you'd be golden. Fumigation was also quite popular for smoking the pests out.

The Victorian Bulb Craze (Yes, Again)

Flowering bulbs were no stranger to Western Europe by the nineteenth century. Many of the bulbs in cultivation were the descendants of the tulipomania of the eighteenth century. But the practice of forcing plants to grow in an unnatural environment (like under glass) had been around even longer, since the time of ancient civilizations. People of Rome, Athens, and Alexandria forced fruits and veggies out of season, but it wasn't until the 1700s that it became a common practice in Western

Popular Victorian Greenhouse Plants

Herbaceous

Amaryllis
Begonia
Iris
Stock
Tulip
Violet

Hardy-Leaved Plants

Agave
Cycads
Dracaena
Palm
Phormium
Yucca

Hard-Wooded Greenhouse Plants

Abutilon
Acacia
Adenandra
Correa
Daphne
Dillwynia

Succulents

Echeveria
Cotyledon
Crassula
Pachyphytum
Sedum

Citrus

Grapefruit
Lemon
Lime
Orange
Pomegranate

Europe. By the early nineteenth century most desirable bulbs were commercially available at a moderate price, so forcing bulbs was a popular way for middle-class Victorians to bring plants into their homes.

Along with semi-affordable bulbs, special forcing vases were sold in many shops and catalogs, and publications like *Gardening for Ladies* provided instructions on how to force specific bulbs and how to get the right products at the right time. Allium, narcissus, cyclamen, crocus, and tulip were popular choices. And amaryllis became popular again toward the middle and end of the century.

But hyacinths were far and away the most popular bulb in the Victorian era. These bulbs had been popular in Western Europe since the 1700s. Empress Josephine once ordered hundreds of hyacinths be forced at the Palace of Versailles. And of all bulbs, hyacinths were the easiest to force in the Victorian home. Even easier than it is to force them in our homes today! Why? Because Victorian homes were kept at much cooler temperatures than we keep ours today, which hyacinth bulbs prefer. By the end of the nineteenth century, the popularity of the hyacinth outranked even the tulip, which was quite the feat. Thousands of varieties were available and affordable.

Horticultural catalogs were inundated with bulb dealers trying to upsell and outsell their competition. It's not surprising that the market was saturated with scammers. Many times, what was advertised in the mail was not what the buyer received. You might have purchased a rare variety of tulip or lily and instead received some common bulb that wasn't worth the effort to ship. And in an era when you couldn't leave a bad Yelp review, there wasn't much you could do about getting ripped off.

Orchid Fever

Nineteenth-century Europeans were susceptible to erupting into hysteria over every rare, "exotic" plant. Especially those that flowered. And especially those that titillated their prudish sensibilities with a resemblance to sexual organs.

Orchids checked both boxes.

What eventually became known as "orchidelirium," or orchid fever, spread across Western Europe during the nineteenth century. The orchid trade became exceedingly profitable in the 1800s as the wealthy upper and middle classes wanted the latest and greatest rare orchids for their collections. Similar to tulipomania, once the demand went sky high, so did the prices. Also like tulipomania, this obsession with orchids started by accident.

During the first decade of the 1800s, a British naturalist by the name of William Swainson was in Brazil, scouring the landscape for exotic plants to ship home to England. As the story goes, Swainson used cast-off plants as packing peanuts—the Wardian case had yet to be invented—and many of those packing filler plants were orchids that hadn't yet bloomed. Swainson had no idea what he'd done. So, when his crew cracked open the crates back in England, everyone flipped because they were full of orchids that had bloomed on the journey.

Word spread fast. Everyone wanted to see these new exotic flowers that could survive such a long, tumultuous crossing. It was no doubt a magical sight. Then, of course, people wanted to buy the blooms for their personal collections.

You can guess the rest.

Was this delirium similar to what happened with the tulips? Yes. But it wasn't an identical craze. Orchids produced prices unheard of for the nineteenth century. Single orchids fetched thousands of dollars. Collectors sought out the most savvy, seasoned explorers to travel to faraway lands to find new varieties in the hopes that they would secure their place in botanical history by naming a new orchid after themselves. These orchid hunters went far and wide, destroying whatever was in their paths. As long as orchids were brought back home, and some of them were alive, their expeditions were considered a success.

Transporting orchids wasn't easy, either. The explorers that collectors hired to find these rare plants weren't always men of botany. Most were cutting down wide swaths of rain forests and throwing all the orchids they could find in crates, then shipping them back home without much care. And sea water equaled plant death, so as you can imagine, the survival rate for these plants was very, very low. It wasn't until the invention of the Wardian case in 1829 that orchids were able to be transported more safely back to England.

Collectors displayed their prizes in ornate, private orchid houses and hired all kinds of staff to care for them. A twenty-first-century reader might be asking why collectors didn't just propagate their collections and sell them off. But we're talking about the early 1800s here. Orchids are notoriously hard to propagate, as most divisions of a plant need to come from "pups" that grow from the mother plant. With orchids, this process can take decades.

Collectors and orchid hunters built empires off their finds. Take Frederick Sander, for example. The man was literally known as the "Orchid King." Sander had a crew of twenty-four orchid hunters that he would send off into the world to bring orchids back to his farm in St. Albans. And he was eventually named the queen's royal orchid grower.

There is something about the orchid that really winds up the human race. It's easy to get hooked, and the onset of orchidelirium will have you in its clutches before you realize you're on your way to buy another one for your collection.

Victorian Women and Their Plants

Take a stroll through the horticulture section of your public library and note the authors' names. You'll find that most serious books on botany that were published up until the twentieth century were written by white men. There are a handful written by women during the Victorian era, like Cornelia Randolph's *The Parlor Gardener,* but these books are trivial and provided very little new information for the time.

Plant books in the 1800s that were written for women, by women focused on plants within the home. The realm of major collectors was typically reserved for men. In the nineteenth century, women were shut out of almost all natural sciences. It was considered indiscreet and unacceptable for a woman to perform the tasks needed to study most sciences. This was also true for the study of botany, for many reasons but one that was especially ludicrous. Women weren't allowed to study

Linnean botany, which was the predominant school of botanical thought at the time because it was based on the sexual organs of plants.

Can you imagine? As if women don't have sexual organs!

While floral design and botanical sketching was completely acceptable and deemed appropriately "domestic," a woman's research and findings in the realm of horticulture would be quickly shot down by "real" botanists as nothing of scientific import. It was acceptable for women to dabble with plants, but that was all.

This ended up being both a blessing and a curse. The oversight allowed scientifically inclined women to take full advantage of the relative anonymity and to dive into the study of plants and botany without the scrutiny of their male counterparts who ruled the natural sciences. However, it was rare that they were taken seriously, even if their findings were published.

The Victorians also loved to diagnose madness, mania, and insanity when any "irregular" behavior was involved. This was particularly true when it came to plants— and, of course, it ended up being deeply gendered. Men in the sciences wouldn't label a trend as a "mania" until women showed the slightest interest—not even when every plant-collecting man was spending their entire savings searching the globe for the next best orchid or scouring the countryside for new species of ferns.

(Oh, yes, ferns. We haven't touched on pteridomania, have we? The Victorians also were mad for ferns—so much so that entire hillsides of fern species in Scotland and Ireland were wiped clean, and it took decades for these spaces to repopulate.)

But just because they weren't taken seriously doesn't mean that Victorian women weren't recording their findings, regardless of what others thought. And many of them made significant contributions to the advancement of botany.

The women listed below are not singular by any means—and this brief offering is not comprehensive. These women deserve an entire book of their own!

Henrietta Beaufort

Henrietta Beaufort was born in Ireland in 1778 to English and French parents. She had a love for botany and wanted to share that love with children. She published *Dialogue on Botany for the Use of Young Persons* in 1819.

She published her book without illustrations (quite the choice during a time when literally every book on botany had some type of artwork inside). Beaufort hoped that it would spur children to go outside looking for plants instead of simply reading about them while indoors. Of course, her contemporaries thought she was absolutely bonkers for doing so. But the book was a success and introduced thousands of children to the science of botany.

Marianne North

One of the most acceptable ways a Victorian woman could explore her interest in botany was to be a botanical illustrator. Women frequently traveled through the countryside sketching and painting whatever plants they came across. If they had access to a greenhouse or hothouse, they could examine and illustrate more exotic, imported plants.

Marianne North was born in Hastings, England, in 1830 to a very wealthy, land-owning family. Her father was a member of Parliament, which allowed her the opportunity to travel to new places along with him. It also helped that he was friends with the director of the Kew Royal Botanic Gardens, Sir Joseph Dalton Hooker.

North's love for botany and botanical illustrations grew from a hobby into a career. She traveled with her father to Switzerland, Syria, and Egypt, and after he died unexpectedly in 1869, she continued to travel internationally on her quest for new plants to paint. She traveled to North America, Jamaica, Japan, India, Borneo, and Brazil—and she was one of the first to successfully document many plants native to the Amazon rain forest. She became acquainted with Charles Darwin, who asked her to travel to New Zealand and Australia to paint the native plants of those countries.

North was renowned for depicting her plants in their natural environment. By the time of her death in 1890, she was famous across England and had secured a gallery at Kew for her portfolio, which totaled more than 900 paintings.

Margaret Gatty

When Margaret Gatty was staying in Hastings on the sea for her health, she took up collecting seaweed that washed up on the beaches. Her seaweed findings were robust. When she organized her marine-plant knowledge into a book called *British Sea Weeds* in 1872, she had compiled the details of more than two hundred species of seaweed local to Hastings.

Even better, *British Sea Weeds* included a guide for women on how to start their own seaweed collection. The guide included what to wear, how and when to go collecting, and what gear was needed, along with information on how to keep unwanted attention away while collecting.

Beatrix Potter

Yes. That Beatrix Potter. The one known for her enchanting children's books with the gorgeous illustrations that people are still losing it for in the twenty-first century. *The Tale of Peter Rabbit* was enraptured with nature of all kinds, including something called mycology: the study of fungi. She went so far as to develop her own theory on how fungi reproduce through spores, which, having been developed by a woman, was not taken seriously.

She completed a scientific paper, "On the Germination of the Spores of Agaricineae," but it was never published even though she submitted it to the Linnean Society of London. There are conflicting reports on what caused the work to not be published. Some say the paper was rejected outright because she was a woman. The Linnean Society made an official statement, claiming that Potter submitted the paper to the society in 1897 under the name Helen B. Potter, and that paper was subsequently withdrawn roughly a month later. According to the society, she was asked to make amendments but never made them for resubmission.

Nineteenth Century America

During the nineteenth century, people had started collecting plants globally, but the Victorians were the biggest collectors of the time. And even though there was still a healthy dose of competition happening between the United States and England, the United States had fallen behind England in the horticultural department—especially regarding bringing plants indoors and collecting them as a hobby.

The late nineteenth century was a tumultuous time for the United States. It wasn't until the end of the Civil War in 1865 that the concept of Victorian living made its way across the Atlantic and into the lives of Americans. Architecture changed to mimic the trends in Europe. Homes were built in the style and colors of the Gothic Revival, Queen Anne, and Second Empire trends. Indoors, Victorian interior decor trends like heavy window curtains, lush carpets, and dark woods were popular.

Along with all these design fads came the Victorian obsession with collecting plants. From greenhouses to conservatories to parlor gardens, Americans followed the trends pioneered by England decades prior.

The New York Botanical Garden was founded in 1891. A decade prior, American botanist Nathaniel Lord Britton visited Kew Royal Botanic Gardens with his wife and came away convinced that New York City needed a similar space for people to visit and learn about the world of plants and to enjoy nature in the middle of a bustling city.

At the turn of the century, fellow New Yorker Peter Henderson published *Gardening for Pleasure*, which outlined directions for Victorian-era window gardening, as well as greenhouse and conservatory plant care. Buried in the middle of the dense volume is a section titled "Humbugs in Horticulture." Henderson used his platform to describe, in great detail, the swindlers and scammers of the New York City plant trade, including a crew of con artists dubbed the "Blue Rose Men." These men traveled around the neighborhoods of New York City selling common seeds and varieties masquerading as fantastical plants. From blue roses (clever) to strawberry trees, these guys had it covered—complete with faux illustrations.

Not unlike a few websites out there today, eh?

YOUR LEAFY LEGACY:
Five Common Houseplants That Are Particularly Cold-Sensitive

This might have you thinking about that one time you left your expensive ficus too close to a drafty window in the middle of winter and watched it languish. Or maybe you just flashed back to when you sat your great-grandmother's Christmas cactus on top of your radiator, and it went from festive to frail overnight.

Tropical houseplant lovers, gather 'round. There's a solid chance that a healthy percentage of us live in temperate climates, where the temperature fluctuates from very cold to very hot, depending on the season. That's okay! That doesn't mean that you can't have and keep your tropical houseplants successfully. What it does mean, however, is that you have to be mindful of temperature fluctuations in your home, like near cold, drafty windows, doors that open to the outside, and forced-air vents. If those things aren't already on your radar, they need to be ASAP.

There are a handful of popular, tropical houseplants that are particularly sensitive to cold temperatures. If you have one, keep it warm and toasty all year long.

Calatheas

To keep calatheas happy during times of chilly temperatures, you're going to need a heat source, high humidity, and a few key tips.

Even though calatheas love moisture, you need to cut down in the winter while the plant is dormant. Keep the soil damp but not saturated. Set up a small humidifier near your calatheas or set them in a tray of stones and water. Make sure the room temperature doesn't dip below 60 degrees Fahrenheit and keep your plants away from cold glass and drafts.

Native Habitat: *South America—mostly in the Amazon rain forest*

Ficus

Ficus plants have been making dramatic statements in homes for decades. Unfortunately, not everyone knows how to care for their ficus when it gets cold. When the room temperature changes drastically where your ficus lives, it will most likely start dropping leaves. (This is why a lot of people claim that these plants are drama queens.) Keep tabs on the temperature in your home. Don't place a ficus near an air exchange/heating vent, radiator, frequently opened door to the outside, or drafty window that gets cold. These plants are very sensitive to temperature fluctuations, so much so that you might notice a difference after walking it home from the plant shop in a late fall or early spring chill. The plant will need an adjustment period of three to four weeks to acclimate to your home's environment. Don't worry if your ficus drops some leaves. It's totally normal, and it will generate new growth over a period of a few months.

Native Habitat: *India, the Mediterranean, Australia, Asia, and the South Pacific*

Tropical Orchids

Most species of tropical orchids like to live in temperatures that vary between 55 and 85 degrees Fahrenheit. Some won't even be mussed by a short period of cold in the upper 30s. However, a significant period of cold will damage your tropical orchids, especially any time spent in below-freezing temps.

The most important thing is to understand your particular orchid's needs. Know what types of temperatures they can handle—some orchids will die when subjected to any type of cold temperature, while others might bounce back. Many times you won't even know your orchid was damaged by the cold until a few days after exposure. Seedlings and young orchids tend to be more temperature sensitive than mature plants.

Native Habitat: *Globally, in tropical climes*

Tillandsia

Tillandsias, commonly known as air plants, are epiphytic plants that can be found growing up in the trees in tropical places. Like most other tropical plants, they do not like being exposed to temperatures under 60 degrees Fahrenheit. These plants get their nutrients from the moisture in the air, so your biggest challenge during the colder months is keeping the air in your home warm *and* moist. Be aware of any fireplaces and air exchanges like heating vents. Keep away from those cold windows too—remember this one since many people keep their air plants in terrariums on windowsills or dangling in front of the windowpane.

Native Habitat: *West Indies, Mexico, Central America, and the southern United States*

Tropical Pitcher Plants

Even though many tropical and subtropical carnivorous pitcher plants can stay happy if the temperature dips (similar to tropical orchids), any significant cold exposure will cause lasting damage. You might be able to get away with keeping your plants in an unheated garage or basement if they live outside during the summer, but it's best to find a warm, sunny spot in your home for them. As always, keep them away from drafty, cold places. Whatever you do, don't let your pitcher plants get cold enough to freeze.

Native Habitat: *Southeast Asia, Australia, Sri Lanka, Madagascar, and Papua New Guinea*

Plant Your Own Wardian Case

These days, it's relatively easy to find young plants grown in smaller, two-inch pots, which are the perfect size for terrarium planting. The traditional Wardian case was used to grow plants that thrive in high-humidity environments—plants like ferns, mosses, and epiphytes. And while modern, open terrariums are a joy to create, it's even more wonderful to attempt a historically accurate one—with a few updated touches, of course.

You will need:

An Enclosed or Closable Glass Vessel
(Well, we're cheating here. We're not actually going to seal our terrariums.)
This can be a custom piece, a large bottle, a clear jar with a lid, etc. The opportunities are endless. If you're feeling fancy, go out and splurge on a designer vessel.

Plants
The size of the plants will depend on the size of the vessel. You'll probably want to start on the smaller side, so stick with two-inch-container-size plants. A lot of nurseries market these as "fairy plants."

Living Moss
Not the dried, dyed stuff you get from the craft store! You need the real deal if you're going to go all the way. Commit! Get a living sheet of Irish or sphagnum moss. The key here is that it needs to be alive. Anything dried that needs to be rehydrated will start to mold inside your terrarium and kill your plants. Is dried moss cheaper? Yes. Don't fall for it. Go big or get ready for a bunch of dead plants in a bottle.

Indoor Potting Mix
Any general kind will do nicely.

Rocks
For layering in the bottom of the vessel. These are for drainage; they don't have to be pretty.

Loose, Activated Charcoal
You can find this online or at a local pet shop. It usually comes in a resealable bag. You might also find some at your local garden store.

Long, Narrow Tongs and a Spoon
Possibly a wooden dowel the size of a pencil. Depending on the size of the opening of your vessel, these tools could be optional. Most of the time you can use your hand if you can fit it into the opening of the vessel. Unless, of course, you're planting a cactus. Use common sense.

Decorative Stones, Wood, etc. for Finishing Touches
This is where you can get really creative. Broken tile, marbles, and figurines can all come out to play. There are even X-rated terrarium figurines if you want to go wild!

Spray Bottle
Multiuse. Spray your plants and your face. #Moisturize

Instructions:

1. Wash your vessel with hot water and dish soap. You don't want any weird fungi, chemicals, or bacteria killing your plants before they get the chance to thrive. Be proactive.

2. Layer the bottom of your vessel with an inch of rock. This is for aeration purposes and will keep the roots of your plants from sitting in water. It will act as a barrier between the plants and the bottom of the vessel.

3. Add a layer of the activated charcoal on top of the rock. This is a trick used by plant shops around the world to keep fungi and bacteria from growing in containers that don't have drainage holes. Think of it as a DIY water filter for your plants. Even your smallest plant deserves primo water.

4. Sprinkle a thin layer of potting soil to make a base for your plants. This is your platform.

5. Take a step back and consider the design and possible topography of your container. Do you want the plants to sit all at one level? While the plants are still in their plastic grower's pots, slide them around inside the vessel and think about the final product. Or you can just go for it and hope for the best!

6. Gently remove the plants from their plastic pots and snuggle them down into the layer of potting soil. Add more soil around the plants so that the root balls are completely covered in an even fashion.

7. Place larger decorations like stones, wood, etc. For a more polished look, sink them slightly below the surface of the soil.

8. Cover the remaining soil with your living moss. Cover as much or as little of it as you like, depending on your aesthetic.

9. Add any other decorative touches. Get fancy. Or not. Whatever you're into.

10. Water the terrarium thoroughly, wetting all of the new plants. You need to saturate the soil, but don't flood the vessel. Afterward, use a spray bottle to clean up the sides of the glass. The stream feature is very useful for getting rid of any dirt.

After you've completed planting your vessel, leave it open until the water on the foliage has dried. Then close it. Keep a close eye on your creation for the first week or so, noting the changes occurring inside. Look for signs of white, fuzzy mold growing on the plants or soil. To get rid of it, scrape it out with a Q-tip or paper towel and treat the area with a mild fungicide.

Once the terrarium starts creating its own condensation, you won't have to check on it as often. You'll be able to easily tell when this is happening—water droplets will start to collect on the top and sides of the glass. The success of your own Wardian case will be reliant upon how tight the lid is. If your lid is airtight, you will probably only have to water your terrarium every three to four months. If your vessel isn't fully sealed, that's okay—just keep an eye on the dryness of the soil and water only when you notice that condensation within the terrarium has dropped.

YOUR LEAFY LEGACY:

Popular Victorian Houseplants

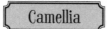

Native to: *China, Japan, Korea, and Indonesia*
Light: *Bright light*
Water: *Water young plants more often. Mature plants need water less frequently. Keep the soil damp but not saturated.*
Soil: *Acidic potting mix that drains well*
Notes: *Plant it slightly higher than the surrounding soil so that the extra water will drain away from the center of the root ball. Also, camellias need lower temperatures at night in order to bloom.*

Aspidistra

Native to: *China, Vietnam, and Japan*
Light: *Indirect to low light tolerant*
Water: *Drought tolerant. Water when the soil is dry all the way through.*
Soil: *Typical potting mix*
Notes: *A great beginner plant, or if you travel a lot or often forget to water your plants*

Kentia Palm

Native to: *Lord Howe Island, between New Zealand and Australia*
Light: *Indirect light. More light will promote new growth.*
Water: *Drought tolerant. Water when the soil is dry all the way through.*
Soil: *Typical potting mix*
Notes: *A great floor plant for those corners that don't get a lot of light.*

Boston Fern

Native to: *North America, particularly Florida*
Light: *Bright, indirect light*
Water: *Keep the soil damp but not saturated.*
Soil: *Typical potting mix*
Notes: *Loves humidity. Turn it every time you water to ensure all sides get light exposure.*

Ficus elastica: The Rubber Tree Plant

Native to: *India*
Light: *Indirect light*
Water: *Water when the soil is dry to the touch. Don't let the soil dry out all the way.*
Soil: *Typical potting mix*
Notes: *If it gets too dry for too long, it will start dropping leaves. Don't fret. The plant isn't dead; it's just throwing a hissy fit.*

Snake Plant

Native to: *Tropical Africa*
Light: *Indirect to low light tolerant*
Water: *Drought tolerant. Water when the soil is dry all the way through.*
Soil: *Typical potting mix or cactus mix*
Notes: *Do not overwater.*

Caladium

Native to: *The rain forests of South America*
Light: *Indirect light. Too much light will burn the sensitive leaves.*
Water: *Keep the soil damp.*
Soil: *Typical potting mix*
Notes: *Must have humidity to thrive. Set the plant in a tray of water or near a humidifier.*

Cattleya Orchid

Native to: *Central and South America*
Light: *Bright, indirect light*
Water: *Only when the potting mix is dry, roughly once a week*
Soil: *Orchid mix*
Notes: *Ventilation and high humidity are key.*

Nepenthes: Pitcher Plant

Native to: *Southeast Asia*
Light: *Bright light*
Water: *Distilled water only. Keep moist.*
Soil: *Mix of peat, sand, perlite, orchid bark, and chopped sphagnum*
Notes: *Grows best in continuously warm, humid, and bright conditions.*

Opuntia

Native to: *Central and North America*
Light: *Bright light*
Water: *Water only when soil is dry all the way through.*
Soil: *Cactus mix*
Notes: *Do not overwater.*

Dracaena fragrans: Corn Plant

Native to: *Tropical Africa*
Light: *Indirect light*
Water: *Water when dry to the touch. Do not let the soil dry all the way through.*
Soil: *Typical potting mix*
Notes: *Great beginner plant. Very forgiving.*

CHAPTER 8

Women Go to Work, and So Do Plants

MOST OF THE TWENTIETH CENTURY (1900–1970)

The 1900s brought indoor climate control for even some of the lower class. Indoor plants became more common and more popular than ever before. During the early 1900s, the art nouveau movement ushered in a shift in interior design. As the middle class climbed the social ranks, plants and fresh cut flowers became an affordable way to decorate indoor living spaces. To meet the demand, florists began selling plants alongside cut flowers, kick-starting a new retail market.

Throughout World War I, houseplants remained a status symbol—so much so that thousands of dollars were spent to decorate the Titanic with palms, ivies, and philodendrons. As it turns out, houseplants had so much staying power that they made it through the Great Depression with their popularity intact.

Wholesale plant nurseries opened across the United States, and after the end of World War II, as women moved into the workplace, houseplants became an expected fixture in the office. By the end of the 1960s, houseplants could be found in almost every indoor public space as well as in every home, no matter the socio-economic status.

Could your work space use some good-looking greenery? The end of this chapter has some great suggestions for plant choices, regardless of whether you work out of a corporate office or from a cute little corner in your home.

1900–1920:
The Excess of the Gilded Age

The Art Nouveau Movement

This international style used natural lines and forms that resembled the types of structures found in plants, flowers, and other objects from nature. Some critics deplored its chaotic and slightly overbearing style, but art nouveau positively took over the design world for a brief period of time. As the style relied heavily on the influence of nature and plants, it frequently featured popular houseplants of the time. Even though its popularity lasted a short time—fizzling out around 1910—art nouveau was extremely influential and had a lasting effect on the design world.

Americans Start to Care About Outdoor Spaces

With the rise of the middle class in the United States came the desire and demand to beautify their outdoor spaces. American cities began to landscape their public space.

Frederick Law Olmsted, who eventually became known as the father of American landscape architecture, died in 1903, but his designs and influence lasted well into the twentieth century.

Olmsted was primarily concerned with the functionality of public space. He designed parks with large, green pastures that acted as a balance against urban sprawl. His influence was so great that cities all over the country began using landscape architects and planners to create large urban green spaces for all to enjoy.

These outdoor spaces were meant to serve different purposes, depending on what people wanted to use them for, and having beautified public areas allowed city dwellers to connect with nature in a way they hadn't been able to before.

A Shift in Decor

The middle class swung upward. As urban areas became more populated, wealthy folks increasingly started moving to the country. Some families made the permanent move, while others purchased second homes for the purpose of getting out of the city and getting fresh air. Advancements in technology—like phone lines in rural places and regular rail service—made these moves possible.

The overboard luxury of the 1800s slid away, but decor was still as important as ever. Monthly design publications like *House Beautiful* and the *New England Architect and Home Builder* encouraged people to fill their homes with greenery. In fact, using plants and cut flowers to decorate the home was touted as an economical way to decorate. After all, plants are much easier to discard when you're tired of them (or if they die) than heavy furniture, fixtures, or mantels.

Fireplaces were the focal points of a room. During the warmer months, they were often decorated with ferns, grasses, and other foliage to create a bringing-the-outdoors-inside look. During the winter months, dried grasses, pods, and flowers provided additional flare, as did berry-producing plants like bittersweet. It was all about connecting with nature.

Plants were frequent players in the dining room as well. Sometimes a florist (professional or amateur!) would re-create a flower bed down the center of the dining table. Mosses, ferns, and small flowering plants like violets and pansies were placed as they would be out in nature, down a forest path perhaps.

The best part of these dining table designs was that it was common practice for guests to take plants and bouquets home as a souvenir from the evening. Many publications noted that growing plants indoors added to the overall morale of the home. These same publications demanded that the home be a welcoming, cheerful place for all men and young boys to live in so that they might aspire and prosper in their trades (yes, the *New England Architect* went there, along with opining about how bizarre it was that women were "invading" trades that should be reserved for men).

But good, commonsense advice was still being passed around, by botanists, nurserymen, and popular publications—everything from how to treat shock after receiving a plant in the mail to using sulfur matches to get rid of houseplant pests like aphids and fungus gnats.

The Age of Kentia

Kentia Palms were popular all the way through the nineteenth century as part of the crowded domestic jungles that ruled homes during the Gilded Age. But as the world moved into the twentieth century, things started to change. Modern styles dropped the cluttered luxury look and made way for the sleek, elegant lines like those of the Kentia Palm to shine on their own. Photographs of early twentieth century residences show that these palms were everywhere, from hotels to restaurants to manors to middle-class parlors. The popular Kentia Palm finally found the spotlight it deserved.

Titanic Plants

The year was 1912. The RMS Titanic set sail in early April on the fateful voyage that has been immortalized by historians and pop culture alike.

The Titanic was built to be the biggest and grandest streamliner in history. The interior was luxurious—after all, the ship was constructed and decorated with the best materials the world had to offer—and the luxury decor, of course, included houseplants. Images taken onboard the Titanic before it set sail show plants in corners, on tables, and even climbing up the walls of the Verandah Café and the Palm Court. There were philodendrons and ivy but, mostly, palms *everywhere*. Even in 1912—decades after the Kentia Palm became ubiquitous—indoor palms still signaled luxury. First-class accommodations were laden with foliage decoration. Don't go looking for it in second or third classes, though—you won't find a single plant.

Beyond the luxurious plant decorations, a large number of other plants, including product from Benary, the famous seed company, were on the Titanic for passage to the United States. The ship's cargo manifest included a very expensive palm tree order headed from the famous Rochford family nursery in England to a family in

Philadelphia, an order which obviously never made it to its destination. And all the Benary seeds went down with the ship, too, but in 2010 four hundred packets of Benary begonia seeds were found in an airtight shipping container in the undersea wreckage, twelve thousand feet under in the Atlantic Ocean. The company decided to see if the seeds would germinate—and they did! More than three thousand plants were produced from those seeds, which have been coined the "Titanic Begonia." These cultivars are extremely hard to find, but if you have the time and the energy, it's possible to bring a little bit of Titanic houseplant history into your own home.

World War I (1914–1918)

When the United States and European world powers entered World War I, the houseplant industry suffered. Up until the start of the war, the plant industry had relied heavily on horticultural publications as their main source for retailers and collectors. The lack of interest and available space in publications for ads led to a tapering of houseplant availability. Houseplants (and the publications that pushed them) simply couldn't compete with the news coming in from the front.

Plant societies began to struggle and many of them barely stayed afloat during this time.

Houseplants were around, but they took a dutiful back seat.

1920–1940

Potted Plants Hit the Market

By the late 1920s, plants intended to be grown indoors were broadly affordable and readily available on the retail market for the very first time. In the early 1920s in the United States, one of the first "large-scale" nurseries to market houseplants and distribute them nationwide was Monrovia, in Southern California. They're still around and very, *very* popular today. Not too far away, at the same time, the society that would become nationally known as the American Begonia Society was taking off in Long Beach, discovering new information about different varieties and cultivation methods. Similarly, the American Amaryllis Society was formed around this time, publishing its first yearbook in 1934.

Cacti and succulents were exceptionally popular, as were flowering bulbs. As you've learned, flowering bulbs had been popular since the 1700s, but succulents and cacti were relatively new on the hobbyist scene. They had been great favorites of serious collectors for hundreds of years, but the general public didn't catch up until after the war.

Books like A. D. Houghton's *The Cactus Book* taught thousands of people the secrets of caring for succulent plants, which is completely different from caring for plants from the tropics. These books also contained information on individual succulent varieties and even how to grow them from seed, which can be quite difficult for even seasoned succulent and cacti owners.

Indoor Winter Gardens

Between 1920 and 1940, architecture trends began to highlight the relationship between nature and urban developments. This was especially true in Europe, where indoor gardens started popping up everywhere and plants and flowers were once again heavily featured in interior decor—particularly in the winter. These so-called "winter garden" living spaces typically had two big glass walls, which turned the living space into a terrarium as well as giving the owners a magnificent view of the outdoors.

The Great Depression

During the Great Depression (1929–1939), an interesting thing happened in the houseplant world. There was an uptick in interest in indoor cultivars. This helped many nurseries and plant businesses scrape by and kept plant societies operational during the massive economic downturn.

Domestic life had changed, and so, too, did the houseplant trade. Conservatories and greenhouses were no longer a requirement to flaunt your expensive plant collection, thanks to the advancements in climate control and insulation. Newer houses were built with better heating and bigger windows—helpful for keeping indoor plants alive. Houseplants became a hobby across all classes, which meant that the market rose, but not across the board. Just because the houseplant industry made it through the Depression doesn't mean that the grand estates and fancy conservatories did. Those expensive greenhouses were the first things to go when the upper class started pinching pennies. Massive collections of rare plants fell into neglect, resulting in many cultivars being lost during this time.

1940–1960

World War II

During World War II, people in the United States shifted back from caring for plants inside the home for pleasure to caring for utilitarian plants. Even though cut flowers were still a staple in many homes, "victory gardens" took precedence.

When food rations were hard to come by and no one really knew what news the next day would bring, the government of the United States encouraged people to grow their own vegetables. These victory gardens took a little weight off the demand for imported foods from outside the country and left more exportable goods for the troops overseas. The victory garden campaign was a massive undertaking for the United States Department of Agriculture. Pamphlets were printed explaining exactly how to start a veggie garden, what plants were best, and how to plan out specific types of gardens depending on how much land you had. Folks took to it in droves, many looking for any way to support the cause while their loved ones were on the front lines.

Only the easiest-to-care-for houseplants remained popular during this time.

Miracle-Gro

Miracle-Gro, the fertilizer brand of our forefathers and one that remains popular (yet controversial) among modern houseplant owners today, came on the market around 1950. The idea for the product came about in 1944 when the developer, Horace Hagedorn, chatted with famed nurseryman Otto Stern about the issues Stern had been having shipping plants. There were a lot of problems, and so they tried their hands at making a fertilizer that would help plants bounce back quickly from shipping stress. It took them a few years, but by the end of the decade Miracle-Gro was ready to take the horticulture world by storm as a plant cure-all.

The First Suburb

After World War II, returning veterans needed abundant affordable housing. On Long Island, a building company named Levitt & Sons planned a community that would provide just that. Built between 1947 and 1950, Levittown, New York, became the country's first official, mass-produced suburban community. The plan was quickly reproduced all over the country.

The ranch- and cottage-style home models quickly became synonymous with postwar America. Even though Levittown's racially discriminatory practices were quite obvious and widely criticized (only white people were allowed to buy in their communities), the model boomed. Soon, a related cookie-cutter style of decor was everywhere and would become a staple among the middle class. Houseplants were part of that decor, but any greenery was carefully chosen and placed to not look messy or cluttered. Bor-ing.

Women in the Workplace

In the postwar era, houseplants once again spiked in popularity, and a surprising factor in that spike was more women entering the workforce and bringing plants along with them. By 1950 women were 30 percent of the entire workforce in the

United States, and many of these women brought plants with them into their work spaces. From small desk plants to large floor plants, houseplants made their way into offices and eventually became an expected element of office decor.

The United States Moves Ahead of Europe

For decades, the United States remained behind Europe when it came to the houseplant trade. But by 1950, American advancements in boiler heating and access to a much wider variety of climates allowed the United States to creep ahead both in the practice and in the theory of houseplant cultivation. Most of the literature about houseplants in the middle of the twentieth century came from publishers in the United States. These books were marketed to the retail consumer of houseplants, not just the botany fanatic. The language was clear and easy to understand, with simple-to-follow instructions and photos to boot.

Not to be outdone, the five-month-long 1951 Festival of Britain highlighted thousands of tropical plants all throughout the exhibition halls alongside revolutionary interior design, kicking off renewed interest in houseplants in England.

1960–1970

The 1960s brought with it the middle and the end of the midcentury modern movement in the design world. Everything was sleek and sexy, and houseplants had to fit that mold too—and boy did they ever. Homes had large, open living rooms with clean lines. Big floor plants fit right in, and so did any other plant that looked even a little bit sculptural.

Popular television shows were an effective selling tool for certain design styles. Shows like *I Dream of Jeannie, Leave It to Beaver,* and *The Brady Bunch* all displayed houseplants in the current, popular fashion. These time capsules show that there were plenty of snake plants, philodendrons, and dracaenas to go around.

Other pop-culture houseplants included Audrey II from the original *Little Shop of Horrors* film, released in 1960. Written by Charles B. Griffith and directed by Roger Corman, this original take on the infamous human-eating houseplant made its debut to marginal success—unlike the 1980s remake, which found a cult following.

Five Popular Floor Plants from the 1960s That Just Kept Giving (and We Still Love Them Today!)

Monstera deliciosa

The *Monstera deliciosa* is a plant that was very popular in the 1960s, and for good reason. It was projected by *Architectural Digest* in 1952 to be "the aspidistra of tomorrow."

Guess they were right!

It's an easy-to-care-for plant that is absolutely gorgeous, and it takes up a lot of space if you let it. It can live in a variety of different light conditions but grows best in indirect light. Too much sun and you'll have a sunburned plant. The more indirect light it's getting, the faster it will grow.

Water it when the soil is dry one inch from the surface. You can judge this by sticking a finger in the soil—one knuckle is roughly one inch. Mist your plant multiple times a week if you can.

When repotting, keep in mind that an *M. deliciosa* will grow into the size of the pot you give it. If you want to keep it smaller, let it get root bound. If you want it to grow bigger, give it more space.

Native Habitat: *Southern Mexico and Central America*

Aglaonema

All varieties of *Aglaonema* are pretty much foolproof. All they need, mostly, is indirect light and water when the surface of the soil is dry. While these guys are technically low-light tolerant, the color variation in the leaves will be stronger if the plant is given more light.

These plants are also known to be very forgiving if you forget to water them for a period of time.

As the plant ages, it will keep its upright growing pattern, and eventually the stems will get very cane-like.

Native Habitat: *Asia and New Guinea*

Ficus elastica "Burgundy Bush"

The burgundy leaves on this guy are just incredibly stunning. This is a must for plant lovers who are obsessed with dark foliage but want a plant that will take up floor space.

The care requirements are roughly the same as other ficus plants, but the "Rubber Tree" is known to be more forgiving, similar to the ficus "Audrey."

These plants can tolerate bright to indirect light and should be turned every time you water them so that they grow straight and don't get a sunburn on their leaves.

Water thoroughly when the soil is dry one inch from the surface.

Native Habitat: *India*

Dieffenbachia

These plants are similar to aglaonemas in care and practice. They're known for their sustainability and for their ability to take up solid real estate in the corner of a room.

The more light they get, the bolder the colors will be. Water when the soil is dry to the touch.

Native Habitat: *The Caribbean islands and South America*

Schefflera

This one is well known as the "Umbrella Tree." This is a popular floor plant because it is easy to care for and can grow quite tall if you let it.

Indirect light is great for these plants. If they don't get enough light, they get leggy and droopy looking. Only water when the soil is dry on the surface—scheffleras like to dry out a bit in between waterings, so don't be heavy handed.

Native Habitat: *Taiwan*

YOUR LEAFY LEGACY:
The Best of the Best Office Plants

If we're going to be working from a cubicle, or any mundane office space, we want plants, right? Right. As any plant-shop employee will tell you, one of the most common customer questions is what plants are best for their office.

"I need a plant that I can leave on the weekends ... and when I go on vacation ... and when I work from home sometimes."

It's not an easy ask. After all, plants do need light, water, and attention. Most offices have poor lighting, and employees are only there during certain hours. Before we go any further, know that those big fluorescent lights that are always on in your office won't make up for not having any windows. It's better than nothing, but don't expect a succulent or cactus to survive if it only has bad office lighting to perform photosynthesis with. Yikes.

Now that we got that out of the way, yes, it's possible to have plants in your office that will survive a certain amount of neglect. Take a look at this list, get your Google on, and then run to your favorite plant shop. These translate to the home office as well!

Pothos

There are all kinds of pothos to choose from: 'N Joy, Pearls and Jade, Neon, and the list goes on. In fact, the "collect 'em all" mentality is one of the best parts of this plant's cult following. The pothos is a drapey plant that looks fabulous coming down off a bookshelf or cascading from a hanging planter in the corner of an office.

Indirect light is best, and you should water weekly. The leaves will start to curl on the edges when it is thirsty. It can tolerate a lower light, but if you want vibrant coloring on your leaves, stick with indirect.

Native Habitat: *Southeast Asia and the Solomon Islands*

Aloe Vera

Aloe vera will always have a place in the home as a useful, gorgeous addition to a full-sun spot on a table or shelf. It has a minimal, compact shape and super easy care requirements. These classic plants are easily identifiable by their plump, ridged leaves and distinct shape. To live a successful existence, aloe vera needs direct or bright, indirect light. Do not overwater this plant. Water only when the soil is extremely dry. Aloe vera will begin to rot when overwatered. Make sure your office has a window if you're going with this plant!

Native Habitat: *Africa, Madagascar, and the Arabian Peninsula*

Snake Plant

Yes, there are just as many varieties of snake plants as there are pothos. It's fun to collect them all, but an all-time favorite for the office is Bantel's Sensation.

This snake plant's coloring is truly unique. While it maintains the upright structure of the more traditional varieties, Bantel's Sensation has white-striped leaves that will have your friends fawning over your new office mate.

It's pretty, but that doesn't stop it from being a steadfast survivor that is virtually summer-vacation proof. It's low-light tolerant for a period of time but will thrive and produce new growth when it is exposed to bright, indirect light. Water it when the soil is dried through. Do not overwater.

Native Habitat: *Bantel's Sensation is a greenhouse-grown cultivation, but its family comes from western Africa.*

Spider Plant

Sometimes spider plants get a bad rap as being difficult to care for. That's just because there's a lot of misinformation out there about their care. Once you get a few fundamentals down, it'll be smooth sailing for you and your spider plant office mate.

One of the most common issues with spider plants is something called water stress. Similar to peace lilies, spider plants freak out when they are overwatered or under-watered. Even though they need a significant amount of humidity, these plants don't like their roots to sit in water. If the leaves are turning black or brown, that's a sign of overwatering. If the tips of the leaves are dry, crispy, and brown, you're under-watering.

Just keep an eye on it. The key to successful spider-plant rearing seems to be observation without a heavy watering hand, which makes it a good contender for an office plant.

Native Habitat: *Tropical regions of Africa, Asia, and Australia*

ZZ Plant

Zamioculcas zamiifolia, more commonly known as the "ZZ Plant," is one of the most sought-after office plants because of its hardy reputation. Aside from death by overwatering, these plants are pretty difficult to kill.

There are multiple varieties on the market these days, from plants with jet-black foliage (Raven) to curly leaves (Zenzi) to dwarf (Zamicro).

ZZ Plants don't need a ton of light to perform photosynthesis, so it's the perfect plant for those awkward, small spaces in your office. Water only when the soil is dry through. Do not overwater! This one is a slow grower, so if you're looking for a lot of action from your office plant, this one isn't for you. On the other hand, if you need a plant that will stay the same size for many years, look no further.

Native Habitat: *Drylands of eastern Africa*

Echeveria

Echeveria is one of the largest genera of succulents and is native to Central America. It grows outward from a center point, making a rosette that rarely gets larger than six inches across.

There are more than one hundred species of echeveria in all kinds of colors, from pink to green to almost black. If you have a nice sunny window in your office, go with these cute little guys!

These succulents need bright, direct light and minimal watering to survive. Only water when the soil is dried all the way through. Do not overwater! Once a succulent has been overwatered, it will struggle to regain its health.

Native Habitat: *Mexico and Central and South America*

Tillandsia

There are hundreds of varieties of tillandsia, or air plants, that have adapted to unique environments like rain forests, deserts, and lowlands. Because they are epiphytes, air plants grow without being rooted in soil, which makes them perfect for office spaces of all sizes. They're also slow growers, so you don't have to worry about your air plant outgrowing your space.

Air plants need bright, indirect light. Keep them away from direct light, as they'll dehydrate and die under the exposure of too much hot sun.

There's a great array of watering recommendations out there, but I recommend watering your air plants once a week. Soak the plant upside down for fifteen to twenty minutes, then set it on a towel to dry. Don't put it back in its spot until it's totally dry, or you'll find it rotting from the inside out.

If soaking isn't the path for you, try misting your air plants daily to supply them with the adequate amount of moisture to thrive.

Native Habitat: *West Indies, Mexico, Central America, and the southern United States*

Dracaena

Dracaenas can be found in homes and businesses all over the world. People love them because they're affordable, easy to care for, and take up quite a bit of space. There are many varieties, like Lemon Lime, that will bring a pop of color to a boring office.

Yes, these plants are easy to care for, but if you put one in too-hot sun or don't water it enough, the edges of the leaves will start to turn brown and crispy. Put this plant in bright, direct or indirect light and give it regular, weekly waterings. Water when the soil is dry one inch from the surface.

Native Habitat: *Africa and South America*

Philodendron "Lickety Split"

This philodendron can add interest to any corner of your office. It's retro, and that's why people love it so much. The luscious green leaves split in a fun way, making each leaf unique. This plant is extremely resilient and can maintain its beauty over a slight period of complete neglect. Give it at least indirect light and water when the soil is dry on the surface.

Native Habitat: *Brazil*

CHAPTER 9

Trends, Poachers, and $20,000 Houseplants

THE MODERN AGE (1970–PRESENT)

T hat brings us to the modern era—from the macramé plant-holder craze of the 1970s to the orchid mania of the 1990s and on to "plantfluencers" today. Plants can now be sourced from just about anywhere in the world and from all kinds of purveyors—from outlets as mundane as Walmart to specialty online collectors and fancy-schmancy boutique shops. Fantastic, right?

Unfortunately, there's a dark side to our current plant fever: it has led to a botanical black market and plant-poaching culture. Garden-variety criminals are driving up the prices of certain "rare" plants, stealing from conservatories and private collections and reselling their loot for big bucks. But it's not all bad news. This chapter will also include a section on the most fascinating—and budget friendly!—modern houseplants and how to care for them. We'll also have a serious conversation about the most commonly poached and stolen houseplants and how to avoid being scammed.

The 1970s

The 1970s was a big decade for houseplants. Like the hairstyles, '70s plants were bigger, funkier, and definitely wilder. Rebelling against the status quo of the tight, tidy '60s plants, '70s houseplant trends went berserk. Vines climbed up walls, and plants potted in containers littered every surface. The name of the game was indoor jungle. Tropical plants of all kinds were in demand, as were small, compact succulents and cacti—and macramé hangers had their time to shine.

Houseplants were part of everyday life. Just about every household had at least one houseplant—they were as common as a toaster or a coffee pot, and people generally knew how to take care of them. Horticultural information was commonplace. PBS aired James Crockett's *The Victory Garden*, which ended up being the longest-running gardening program in the United States. Crockett spent just as much time talking about outdoor gardening as he did about houseplants. He published a bestselling book, *Crockett's Indoor Garden,* to boot.

In the mid-1970s, multiple editions of *The Gardener's Catalogue* were published and became the go-to publication for all amateur gardening knowledge, including about houseplants. The book had 320 pages and was decidedly oversize. It touted itself on the cover as "the most important gardening tool since the watering can" and was printed on vintage-looking paper to add to the vibe. It included a source section for every major metropolitan area in the United States, complete with contact information. And the illustrations were especially titillating. Even *Better Homes and Gardens* jumped on the indoor plant book scene with *Favorite Houseplants and How to Grow Them*, a ninety-six-page reference guide to popular plants.

Chances are, if you lived through the 1970s in the United States, you had some kind of knowledge or opinion about houseplants.

April 22, 1970: The First Earth Day

Americans lived a very dirty existence brought on by the Industrial Revolution. Major industry produced a seemingly infinite amount of pollution that was constantly released into the air, soil, and public water sources. It was rare that anyone gave a second thought to the impact of this pollution on the environment (or even the impact on humans). The streets were dirty. The rivers were dirty (and frequently caught fire in urban areas). And politicians turned a blind eye to oil spills and other man-made disasters in the name of the almighty dollar.

Eventually, small groups of environmentalists started forming across the country. In 1962, Rachel Carson's *Silent Spring* was published and raised rapid awareness of the damage being done to our planet.

One of the first politicians in the United States to take up the issue of pollution was Senator Gaylord Nelson from Wisconsin. After a major oil spill in Santa Barbara, California, in 1969, he felt that the issue could no longer be ignored. Taking inspiration from the Vietnam War protests, he hoped that people would take up the pollution issue with the same enthusiasm and results.

Eventually, after many smaller events and help from younger activists, Nelson and his supporters established a nationwide Earth Day. The media caught on, and the rest is history. More than twenty million people participated in the first Earth Day. By the end of the decade, the Environmental Protection Agency (EPA) had been created and the Clean Air Act and Clean Water Act were passed, along with the National Environmental Education Act.

As it turns out, there were millions of people who cared about the environment and the green things of the world, which perhaps shouldn't have been a surprise considering how popular and beloved houseplants were at the time.

Terrariums

You wouldn't be wrong if you wanted to call the 1970s the "Victorian Era, Part Deux." Tropical plants were abundant, and so were terrariums. The garden book market was saturated with how-to books that outlined everything you'd need to know about planting a terrarium of your own. From glassware to tools to soil recommendations, these books had it covered. Bottle terrariums were particularly popular alongside acrylic, Lucite standing terrariums that it seemed everyone just had to have. Seventies terrariums would be stuffed to the hilt with ferns, succulents, orchids, and air plants. Mosses and creeping ficus plants grew abundantly. This terrarium craze was nowhere near as ubiquitous as it was during the Victorian era, but it was nostalgic enough to make a lasting impact. Houseplants of the 1970s are inextricably linked with ficus trees, philodendrons, and terrariums.

Popular Plants of the 1970s

Philodendrons

There are 480 varieties of philodendrons from tropical climes all over the world. They grow in all shapes, sizes, and directions. Some have large leaves and grow upright, some are climbers, and some stay small and compact. There's a philodendron out there for everyone, and plant lovers of the 1970s were no exception.

From split- and heart-leaf plants to the more upright Xanadu, philodendron varieties were everywhere, relatively easy to care for (indirect light, water when the soil is dry), and they really complemented the house-jungle vibe that was so popular during this time.

Inch Plant • *Tradescantia zebrina*

This inch plant has gorgeous silver and purple shimmery foliage that sparkles in the sunlight. It's famous for rapidly growing into any container that it's planted in (it *inches!*). This babe is a vining wonder that brings a little extra dimension into a large plant collection. It's also relatively simple to care for—bright, indirect light and water when the soil dries through.

Native Habitat: *Mexico*

Umbrella Tree • *Schefflera actinophylla*

This tree took up the corners of possibly thousands of living rooms during the 1970s. If you're lucky, the umbrella tree can grow up to fifteen feet tall when kept indoors as a houseplant. It has big, green compound leaves that split into leaflets, which gives it the effect of an umbrella. This schefflera likes bright, indirect light and should be watered when the soil is dry to the touch.

Native Habitat: *Australia and New Guinea*

Spider Plants • *Chlorophytum comosum*

This might be the most '70s plant of the whole list. The spider plant is also famous for being pretty bulletproof when it comes to neglectful owners. Bright to indirect light and a good dose of water every now and then will suit this plant just fine. It also produces pups, or baby plants, which are great to share with friends.

Native Habitat: *Tropical Africa, Asia, and Australia*

Ficus

Ficus trees have been making dramatic statements in homes for a century or more, but they really had their moment in the 1970s. These days, a lot of people think that a ficus can be a total beast to care for, which is why by the 1990s many people started buying fake ones. Can they be temperamental? Of course. Some varieties like *Ficus benjamina* 'Danielle' are notorious for dropping all their leaves if the breeze off the ceiling fan hits them wrong. But with enough bright light and a good soak about once a week, your ficus will thrive. They are, however, sensitive to temperature change and to being moved around. Your best bet will be to find a good place for the plant to live, plop it down, and rotate it each time you water it.

Native Habitat: *India, the Mediterranean, Australia, Asia, and the South Pacific*

The 1980s

Ah, the '80s. The Decade of Decadence. Home decor was dominated by chic, slick interiors. Straight lines, pastels, and privacy glass were everywhere. People wanted their stuff to look like the fanciest, newest thing, regardless of the cost. Gone were the cluttered, busy homes of the 1970s. The home-jungle was replaced by two or three strategically situated, structural-looking plants that delivered visual impact as standalones.

But what caused this shift? Perhaps those big, demanding plant collections grew to be too much. After all, it can be quite time-consuming to take care of the dozens of plants that made up those 1970s collections. The houseplant-buying demographic of the 1980s became yuppies in their 20s and 30s who wanted the newest trends without all the upkeep.

The Mall Jungle

While homes became a sleek minimalist paradise, shopping malls were booming— absolutely teeming with consumers. These suburban malls became oases for after-school teens and weekend professionals with high credit limits. For two decades, the mall was the place to be. Developers built them as big-time places for big-time commerce.

The corridors were crammed with fountains, benches, and food courts that overflowed with planters full of greenery. Skylights let in natural light, which gave the impression of some kind of outdoor/indoor shopping rain forest, complete with tropical plants. All across the United States you could find similar-looking shopping malls—all imprints of one another.

Popular 1980s Mall Plants

Ficus benajmina 'Danielle'
Bright light, water when the soil is dry to the touch.
Native Habitat: *India, the Philippines, and Malaysia*

Dracaena fragrans
Indirect light, water when the soil is completely dry.
Native Habitat: *Tropical Africa*

Yucca
Bright light, water when the soil is completely dry. Drought tolerant.
Native Habitat: *North and Central America*

Snake Plants
Indirect to low light, water when the soil is completely dry. Drought tolerant.
Native Habitat: *Tropical Africa*

Pothos
Indirect to low light, water when the soil is completely dry. Drought tolerant.
Native Habitat: *Asia and the Solomon Islands*

Parlor Palm
Indirect light, water when the soil is dry to the touch.
Native Habitat: *Central America and Mexico*

Bromeliads
Technically an epiphyte. Indirect light, water when the soil is dry to the touch.
Remember to fill the plant's reservoir (the middle of the plant) with clean water.
Native Habitat: *Tropical North and South America*

Crotons
Bright to bright, indirect light. Water when the soil is dry to the touch.
Native Habitat: *Indonesia, Australia, and Malaysia*

Showy Plants

During the 1980s plants were supposed to look good and fit the design aesthetic, no matter the care requirements. Luckily, most of those plants that fit the design trends of the time were relatively easy to care for. These plants looked great as standalone pieces in the home. A nice, big floor plant tucked into a corner or a small fern perched on the glass coffee table did the trick.

Self-Watering Pots

Versions of self-watering containers have been around since the great ancient civilizations and their irrigated outdoor pots. The technology ebbed and flowed throughout the decades, but by the 1980s almost every office with plants had some type of self-watering container. After all, this was the decade of working smarter, not harder.

Similarly, hydroponics became popular with hobbyists trying their hand at growing veggies and houseplants in water. However, this was a relatively niche trend.

As young professionals became more successful, they no longer wanted to worry about keeping plants alive at home. They were too busy staying late at the office, hustling for the next dollar, a culture that as the '80s turned into the '90s kicked off the next big plant trend—one that had absolutely nothing to do with living, growing plants.

The 1990s

There is *so* much to say about the 1990s—and not just about houseplants. It's sometimes difficult to really take in the travesty of '90s design. Tray and popcorn ceilings, awful color palettes, and wild window treatments plagued all levels of home design, from the most elite to mass-market. But while some design and decor choices were questionable, many houseplant owners in the 1990s—whether they were hard-core collectors or spontaneous purchasers of an aloe or palm tree—cared about the science behind their plants.

Home and garden publications were on top of it. The push was on for more greenery in homes. Publications printed scientific studies showing that we, as humans, live calmer, more efficient, and more satisfying lives when we coexist with plants in our living spaces. Guides described how keeping plants is therapeutic and a meditative practice that benefits our mental and physical health. Studies were released showing that houseplants clean the air inside our homes, during a time when air pollution was at an all-time high across the globe.

Houseplants were pushed as a cure-all for the modern condition, and consumers gobbled them up. With all of those plants came the need for information on the keeping and care of them. Almost every home and garden publication put out guides on how to incorporate houseplants into homes and offices. These guides outlined watering and light requirements for various popular houseplants. Care charts outlined how to handle plant care in all types of situations, from being away for the weekend to lengthy vacations.

The people learned, and the plants thrived. Houseplants reigned supreme.

Plastic Plants, Plastic Flowers

Even though houseplants dominated the 1990s, we must take a moment to appreciate a particularly bizarre "houseplant" trend that we haven't been able to shake since: plastic. With the sharp spike in houseplant interest came a very real consumer peak in artificial, plastic plants.

Where there is a trend for caring for living things, there's always a sidetrend that promises to be easier with less maintenance (pet rocks, anyone?). Houseplants are no exception.

The 1990s weren't the first emergence of fake houseplants. In fact, they've been around for a very long time. There are historical documents showing that the Chinese started making fake flowers from silk 1,700 years ago. Romans used malleable wax to create faux flowers and plants. The trend made its way through most European empires until it found its way to the Americas, where it ebbed and flowed until the bombshell that was the 1990s.

These '90s fake plants were made of plastic fibers molded and pressed into maybe-from-a-distance realistic houseplants. Ficus trees and ivies were heavy hitters when it came to the faux plant game. While they were desirable and trendy at first, these posers quickly collected dust, dirt, and cobwebs and were a complete nightmare to keep clean. As the trend faded, it's safe to say that most plastic plants were tossed out and made their way to the local landfill, like most fast fashion and design.

153

Time Warp: Orchid Fever, 1990s Style

The 1990s decor style was a bit … busy. With that came a yen for houseplants that grew in symmetrical, straight lines. A sort of calm in the midst of chaos. Enter the orchid. Throughout history orchids have been an intoxicating obsession to many, from royalty to penniless explorers willing to risk it all for that one rare specimen.

Through a ton of work that spanned centuries, orchids—mostly phalaenopsis— were finally affordable to the common buyer. Plants that were once only available to the ultrarich were now on grocery store shelves, thanks to cloning and breeding technology in Asia.

It took us something like five hundred years to figure out how orchids reproduced. Early botanists swore that orchids were fertilized by bird sperm because orchid seeds were so small and difficult to see. In the 1970s, Dutch orchid growers started mass-producing phalaenopsis orchids through cloning for the cut-flower trade. By the end of the decade, the price of this easygoing orchid was almost affordable.

And then Taiwan entered the game. They used a totally different cloning technique that brought plants to maturity in a short amount of time. Taiwan's breeding program was spitting out millions of orchids every year at an insanely low wholesale price. This saturated the market and edged out almost every successful grower worldwide. With that, the $5 grocery store orchid was born.

The Lies the Media Told You about NASA

Just before the 1990s, NASA scientist Bill Wolverton released a report known as the NASA Clean Air Study. The study implied that certain houseplants had the potential to filter pollutants from the air. The report's central findings recorded how certain plants absorbed volatile organic compounds, or VOCs. There was great interest in whether certain plants could indeed remove the toxins from the air inside our homes. VOCs are more common than you might think. Benzene, formaldehyde, and trichloroethylene can all be found in drywall, house paint, nail polish, and air fresheners. Who wouldn't want to breathe in fewer of those chemicals?

NASA's Clean Air Study Plants

Aloe vera *(Aloe barbadensis miller)*

Banana Plant *(Musa acuminata)*

Bamboo Palm *(Chamaedorea seifrizii)*

Chinese Evergreen *(Aglaonema modestum)*

Dracaena deremensis "Janet Craig"

Dracaena deremensis "Warneckii"

Dracaena fragrans

Dragon Tree *(Dracaena marginata)*

Dracaena trifasciata "Laurentii"

English Ivy *(Hedera helix)*

Gerber Daisy *(Gerbera jamesonii)*

Heartleaf Philodendron *(Philodendron cordatum)*

Peace Lily *(Spathiphyllum)*

Potted Mums *(Chrysanthemum morifolium)*

Pothos *(Epipremnum aureum)*

Spider Plant *(Chlorophytum comosum)*

Weeping Fig *(Ficus benjamina)*

Was there truth in that study? Absolutely. However, the media in the United States ran with the story, then blew it all out of proportion. Many investigative journalists and scientists have since attempted and somewhat succeeded in debunking the study, specifically taking issue with the fact that NASA never actually set out to see how these plants would perform in normal houses. These experiments were performed inside sealed test chambers—a key detail that was left out when the study was covered.

But this didn't stop people from buying into the too-good-to-be-true promises of "the NASA plants that will clean your air." Plants from the published list flew off the shelves of retailers and greenhouses.

Though they may not provide *all* the media-hyped air-purifying benefits, having houseplants in your home does provide benefits other than mental and aesthetic stimulation. The American College of Allergy, Asthma, and Immunology found that many of the plants on the NASA list, particularly English Ivy, are great at ridding the air in homes of mold spores.

The bigger a plant's leaves, the more work it does. So, consider this permission to go out and buy that huge monstera you've been dying to get your hands on.

2000–2010

The 2000s were a wild time for houseplants. Hot off the NASA Clean Air Study wave, consumers wanted lots of houseplants, albeit easier ones to take care of to fit in with their busy jobs and lifestyles. Consumers were less interested in the science of the plants and more interested in the ease of care.

Out of Luck? Try Bamboo. Or Is It a Dracaena?

The new millennium brought back a popular houseplant trend from the 1970s: lucky bamboo.

A quick dip into the feng shui trend of the late '90s explains the obsession. Houseplants are a very important component of feng shui, which is an ancient Chinese art of placing furniture and objects in the home in a certain way to promote positive energy.

Poor *Dracaena sanderiana* just got stuck in the middle.

D. sanderiana, also known as lucky bamboo or ribbon bamboo, is a compact species from the *Asparagaceae* family that is native to central Africa. Like the Latin name shows, it is not a bamboo at all. In fact, the name "lucky bamboo" is misleading on all fronts. It's not a bamboo, and it's not native to China, even though it's frequently marketed as such.

The plant is typically sold as cuttings rooted in water, and usually the stalks are woven or tied together to keep the plant compact. If you plant it in a container, however, it will lose its bamboo-like shape and grow more like a traditional dracaena.

There's some misinformation out there that this plant can live in complete darkness. But in order to thrive *D. sanderiana* needs indirect light and for the water to be constantly changed.

Lucky bamboo had one heck of a trip in the early 2000s. It was cheap to grow, so everyone who sold it was making a profit. And the plant appealed to folks who didn't think they could grow houseplants—after all, there was no planter, no soil, just a compact plant sitting in a little bit of water.

Suckers for Succulents

As we moved into the 2010s, succulents, cacti, and terrariums (yes, again) took over. Everything was desertscape as succulents were marketed as the easiest, hands-off houseplant to ever hit the shops. In the design sphere, everything shifted at the same time. Southwest decor was having a moment, and cacti and succulents fit right in. The plants were compact and easy to handle, and they communicated that the owner had a trendy sense of design.

Succulent-themed businesses popped up out of nowhere disguised as "plant nights," where folks would gather at a bar and plant a succulent terrarium, only to be told that all they had to do was mist their succulents every once in a while, and they would thrive.

No. Just, whatever you do, don't mist your succulents. They'll rot.

These arid plants completely saturated the design world. There are tens of thousands of varieties out there to collect, and they're easy to pack up and ship across the country. An online shopper's dream!

The flaw in this succulent scheme is this: These plants need bright light to survive and minimal water. Specifically, for those rose-like echeverias that were so popular during this time, they need bright light to keep from rotting and falling apart. They're not the absolutely foolproof, effortless houseplants they were marketed as, and many succulents and cacti met their unfortunate end during this time.

Urban Farming Comes Inside

The 2010s also saw renewed interest in urban farming. There was an entire PR campaign, Food Not Lawns, that pushed landowners to give up ornamental yards and landscaping in favor of planting edible plants. Utilitarian plants instead of decorative ones—sound familiar? This trend shook the landscaping industry, and edible plants also started popping up in the houseplant market. Dwarf fruit trees like limes, lemons, and pomegranates were popular picks for sunny windows. And the kitchen windowsill herb garden took off for those who wanted their kitchens to look like a Nancy Meyers film.

People wanted plants they could grow indoors and also eat. The hydroponic industry boomed when the technology became so advanced that some systems were essentially plug-and-play.

Murderous Millennials

After the houseplant trend exploded into Victorian-era proportions at the end of the 2010s, the media was dying to dream up an explanation. They landed on blaming millennials. You know, the generation that gets blamed for killing restaurants and movie theaters and any number of industries, along with the traditional life milestones of their predecessors.

Oh, yes. Apparently, millennials would rather have houseplants than children. Multiple publications from *House Beautiful* to the *New York Times* have featured articles about millennials replacing milestones like having kids, buying homes, and getting married with houseplants—mostly making these pared-down life decisions for financial reasons, especially in the United States. In major urban areas, rent is so high that it's almost impossible to pay all your bills and then have money left over for a down payment, a wedding, or extra mouths.

And so, millennials have turned to houseplants for comfort of all kinds. The plant business has been booming, but did the popularity spike come from broke millennials alone? No, not really. If you've learned anything from this book of houseplant history, it's that the popularity of having plants indoors has ebbed and flowed since the beginning of time. Hobbies fall in and out of favor throughout the decades.

So, what is causing the spike this time? It all seems very intense.

It's social media. Facebook. Instagram. TikTok. Snapchat. All of it is problematic in one way or another. It's addictive, it's aspirational, and it's fast. It only takes a few minutes and the right content creator to start a record-breaking trend.

We've all seen those deceptively gorgeous houseplants online. You know, the ones everyone drools over—the glamorous fiddle-leaf figs, gem-like String of Pearls, elegant maidenhair ferns, and cascading rosary vines. They all look amazing in photographs, and just about anyone can fall victim to Instagram plant envy.

Living in a jungle of houseplants looks amazing—and it can be, if you're ready for the task of caring for them. But that effort is almost never shown in the perfectly curated images you see online.

Over the thousands of years of indoor plant cultivation, one of the main threads of appeal is the connection to nature. When you grow a plant indoors, you're coaxing the plant to grow in an unnatural environment (in a container, indoors) where you are the sole caretaker. Cultures all over the world embraced that responsibility and didn't take it for granted. Even the often-frivolous Victorians recognized that they were bringing wild things indoors, and those living things should be respected.

Now houseplants have become purely aesthetic accessories, and over a period of a few years, that connection to nature has been lost. This is a blanket statement that might not be true for every houseplant owner these days—and there are many genuine collectors out there for which the connection to nature is sacred—but many people want houseplants for the photo ops and for the clout. Since 2010, the houseplant industry has grown exponentially because of this. There are now thousands of houseplant shops across the globe that specialize in the indoor cultivation trade. The same can be said about plant nurseries—there are just as many that focus on growing tropical and arid plants for indoors as there are that focus on landscape plants.

Pandemic Plants

The social media houseplant craze coupled with isolation fueled an entirely different type of plant frenzy during the COVID-19 pandemic, one that the plant industry will likely see reverberations from for years to come.

In 2019 the scene was set. A handful of big-time collectors had started to show off their fancy houseplants on social media—plants that were hard to find because of how long it took them to be cultivated from seeds or cuttings. Interest exploded for *Monstera* "Thai Constellation" and any plant that had pink variegation, like the philodendron "Pink Princess." There was the great philodendron "Pink Congo" scam, where plant nurseries were treating regular philodendron "Congos" with ethylene gas (the same gas used to ripen fruit) to turn their new growth bright pink. Thousands of people spent thousands of dollars thinking they were buying something they weren't. Yikes.

And then, all of a sudden, we couldn't leave our homes. For months. The tragic and tumultuous time had a lot of people looking around their living spaces, wondering how they could beautify them.

The answer? Plants.

Demand skyrocketed and supply depleted. Even though many reputable houseplant shops took their retail space online with shipping or contactless delivery, there weren't enough people working in the wholesale nurseries to keep up with the demand. And, of course, it takes plants time to grow.

So, people took the trade to social media and then to the black market, and then suddenly the industry was inundated with scams, criminal theft, and horticultural fraud. A hobby based in nature and sunlight had a new, seedy underbelly.

Prices skyrocketed. Online swap/trade sites were swamped with philodendrons and monsteras, and hoyas sold at auction for top dollar. Plants that used to be easy to find—like pothos—were suddenly so in demand that you couldn't find one at a decent price. Flipping plants for a profit became a common practice.

Rare plants were ripped out of exhibits in botanic gardens and stuffed into pockets. Nurseries were robbed at gunpoint. Online houseplant forums filled with accusations of fraud, price gouging, and theft. A *Monstera albo* that once sold in shops for fifty dollars was being chopped up into one-inch chunks that sold for $200 each—nodes that "might" root. Collectors lined up, masked, around the block for an alocasia that most shops couldn't sell a year prior because the plant was too basic.

In June of 2021 an online buyer in New Zealand shattered the record for the most expensive houseplant bought at auction. After a massive bidding war that teetered on edge in the final minutes, the lucky winner scored a "rare" white variegated *Rhaphidophora tetrasperma* for a cool $19,297. This specific plant had eight leaves and was planted in a five-inch pot. That's almost $2,500 a leaf!

As global restrictions lifted, houseplant prices started to return to normal, but the effects on the industry and its consumers are expected to last for years.

Plant Globalization and Our Impact as Consumers

These days, the best plants are at our fingertips. Gone are the days of simply going to your favorite nursery and picking out a new houseplant. Well, you can still do that, but there are so many more options for purchasing. From local shops to big-box stores to buy/swap groups and social media auctions—you should be able to find the plant you want. Some private collectors are even going as far as to import plants, bypassing the middlemen—the wholesaler, the broker, and the actual retail shop—entirely.

It's a remarkably similar environment to the plant market of the nineteenth century. No, people aren't hiring plant hunters to go chop their favorite philodendron off a tree in Indonesia (okay, there actually might be a chance that this happens), but people can hunt other avenues for their wish-list plants, and some of those avenues are shady business.

Different countries have different import/export laws with all kinds of loopholes that plant fiends have found their way through. The current plant trade works through a complex web of biosecurity and customs regulations. Up until the 1980s it was very easy for plant hunters, collectors, and wealthy people to travel to far-away countries and rip plants from their natural habitats for the sake of science and cultural advancement.

In the late 1970s and early 1980s, the United Nations debated the issue of poaching and the impact on biodiversity. Over the centuries, foreign plants were not only introduced to the greenhouses and conservatories of collectors but also to their outdoor gardens. Plants that ended up outdoors quite often ended up being invasive—some doing massive damage to their new environments. At the time of introduction, these plants were thought of as innocent collector's items. Some plants were even introduced on purpose because botanists thought they would help more than they would harm. Some were gifts from the governments of foreign lands.

But accidents happen. A lot of small-time collectors don't mean any harm when they find their way around import laws to get their dream plant. Or maybe they don't know where the plant came from. Or the dealer was kind of sketchy, but they think it's okay just this one time. Right?

In reality, these small actions have a snowball effect and contribute to turning the houseplant trade toxic.

As a community, we bring plants into our homes and dote on them like they are our children. We, the consumers, fuel an entire horticultural industry that supplies us with tropical, subtropical, and desert plants to keep for our pleasure. It's a massive market that is floating hundreds of thousands of honest, hardworking people who are also passionate about the plant trade. It's the hobby to end all hobbies—one that's been chugging along since the rise and fall of the ancient civilizations. One that takes advantage of the natural world for our own enjoyment.

Can we really claim to be lovers of houseplants and in turn have no respect for the planet they come from or the other people who have worked to bring them to us? It is our responsibility to be thoughtful consumers. We need to be mindful of how we inhabit and interact with the earth and understand the consequences of our actions. We can't propose to be lovers of nature if we are also part of a system that abuses it.

Humans conquer in the name of our own needs and desires. That's how we ended up with houseplants in the first place. It is possible to be a mindful, responsible consumer of cultivated plants as long as you don't put on blinders to the line between celebration and exploitation. The industry has been fraught with scandal, abuse, and irresponsible practices for thousands of years—but that doesn't mean we can't change it for the better.

YOUR LEAFY LEGACY:
Ethical Houseplants

How does rare plant sourcing work?

The houseplant industry is now a booming multibillion-dollar institution, and the sourcing of popular houseplants can be far from ethical.

This is how the houseplant industry works for you as a consumer.

Say you live in a major metropolitan area in the United States. You go to your favorite local plant shop, hoping to score a "rare" houseplant for your collection. Maybe you're on the hunt for an affordable philodendron "Pink Princess" (PPP) or a *Monstera* "Thai Constellation." You get to the shop and are pleasantly surprised when you see a perfect PPP sitting there, almost like it was waiting for you. You snatch it up and don't even flinch when the sales associate tells you that your total is $230 plus tax. That gorgeous pink variegation is worth every cent.

Right?

Five years ago, plant shops couldn't even move them. And now? Now the markup is insane. Almost quadruple what it was in 2019. Who knows? By the time this book hits shelves, some other plant may have come into favor, leaving the PPP in the dust again.

But where does this plant even come from? Are you picturing an elusive philodendron deep in the shadows of a mystical rain forest? It might have been like that once, but now they're grown in a lab, for the sake of continuity. Almost every single PPP on the market has been grown through something called tissue culture, or TC. Every PPP has DNA that determines how much pink variegation each plant shows on its leaves. The only way to duplicate that promised variegation is to harvest the DNA through TC and grow a batch of cloned plants in a petri dish.

But even through TC, that variegation isn't promised. Many of the new baby plants won't show that signature pink at all, so they go in the trash. Only the plants with stable pink variegation move up the ladder to the wholesale greenhouses, where they're bumped from petri dish to tiny pot to small pot until they're ready to distribute to retailers. Because so many of the plants end up without stable variegation, the ones with strong, pink markings become high-dollar plants. It's a classic example of supply and demand.

That local plant shop you love to support does a ton of leg work to get you your plants, lab-grown or not. The plant shop buyer typically works through a broker, who has connections at multiple wholesale greenhouses. Once the orders are in, plants get picked off the greenhouse shelves, sleeved and boxed, and then pushed through a shipping facility where they're put on an 18-wheeler and sent out to your local plant shop and into your hands.

Poaching

As it has been throughout the history of houseplants, poaching is a very real issue. This has become especially true over the past few years, as people have taken up houseplant collecting during the COVID-19 pandemic as never before. The increased business has been welcome for many wholesale greenhouses and small retail businesses that supply houseplants to the public, even if they struggle to keep up with demand. The houseplant boom has also been quite the cash cow for many independent online retailers. Some species of plants saw up to a 4,000 percent increase in price during the pandemic, depending on the seller.

Enter the bad seeds. While there are many of us who innocently buy, sell, and trade houseplants—common or rare—there's a possibility that just as many people are out there trying to run a con.

A quick online search for the latest must-have houseplant will link you to hundreds of independent sellers on Etsy, eBay, and social media. These are all platforms that allow anyone to sell, and with minimal regulations, these sites have easy-to-find back doors and loopholes. Ethical sourcing of houseplants is extremely difficult. Long story short, you really can't reliably trace your plant's origins. It's almost impossible to find out where your little four-inch houseplant came from without going from the seller > broker > wholesale greenhouse > grower > buyer/plant source. Sometimes there are hundreds of people involved. It's hard to unravel.

Ethical houseplants are grown for retail in a few different ways. They can be grown from seed. They can be propagated from a mother plant. They can also be grown via tissue culture in a lab through extracted plant DNA. But these methods are not the only ways plants make it onto the retail scene. An unknown (but thought to be large) percentage of plants being bought, sold, and traded on the independent market—and sometimes on the legit retail commerce market—have been ripped from their natural habitats illegally and sold, either directly to the consumer or to a greenhouse growing operation under false pretenses. The United States Fish and Wildlife Service and the Department of Agriculture confiscate tens of thousands of black-market plants in the United States every year.

The plants that are most in demand, the plants that are driving the market, are what have been dubbed "rare" plants. These plants aren't necessarily "rare" by definition. They were once thriving in nature and easy to find in the rain forests of the world. Now they've become difficult to find in cultivation—hence "rare." These are the plants that are at high risk of being poached from their natural habitats.

Top plants at risk for poaching:

1. Staghorn Ferns
2. Vanda Orchids
3. Begonias
3. Alocasias
4. Hoyas
5. Lady's Slipper Orchids
6. Nepenthes
7. Monsteras
8. Venus Flytraps
9. Tillandsias
10. Cycads

Plant poaching has been a common crime for centuries—with orchids, succulents, carnivorous plants, and cacti all being popular with poachers at different times—and now tropical plants, especially aroid species, are under attack. Considering that some, like the *Philodendron spiritus sancti*, can bring a price tag of $20,000 or more, that makes a lot of sense.

But poaching is devastating to ecosystems and is driving some species toward extinction. Think of it as "mini-deforestation." Countries that are home to extremely diverse ecosystems, collectively called "megadiverse ecosystems," have become hotbeds of plant-poaching activity. Countries like Colombia, Brazil, Peru, Indonesia, and Australia have become targets for poachers. The Republic of the Philippines' Department of Environment and Natural Resources reported that the COVID-19 pandemic has fueled plant poaching throughout the country.

Some governments have buckled down on export regulations, while others have chosen to turn a blind eye. But even with stricter guidelines in place, poachers still find a way to get their hands on plants they can turn around at a higher price. Then, either someone will buy the plant, or it will wither and die. Do you think plant poachers know how to take care of these prized plants? Of course not!

Unfortunately, this is a consumer-driven problem. Supply and demand—that's how it works.

So, how can you, a houseplant collector, help?

Start by asking some questions like the ones on page 171.

YOUR LEAFY LEGACY:

Houseplants for the Modern World

Ficus Audrey

Ficus benghalensis

We're all familiar with the big, showy leaves of the *Ficus lyrata*, also known as the fiddle-leaf fig. But at this point, they're as common as a grocery store succulent. So if you're looking for a large plant with a different look, try a *Ficus benghalensis*, also called *Ficus* "Audrey."

The plant is a close cousin of the fiddle-leaf fig. It's also a real stunner with soft, velvety, elegant leaves that are a bit rounder and smaller than the fiddle-leaf fig's. And the "Audrey" bounces back from looking crummy faster than the fiddle-leaf fig, making it a much more forgiving plant companion.

Native Habitat: *India and Pakistan*

Variegated String of Pearls

Senecio rowleyanus variegata

The variegated String of Pearls is the normal String of Pearls' cool older sister. It's a gorgeous plant—the succulent pearls are variegated in the most delicious-looking fashion. Some owners have said that the plant can grow an entire strand of the pearls that are white!

Just like its sibling, this variety of String of Pearls can be temperamental. It needs bright light, and that is a nonnegotiable aspect of having this plant and keeping it alive.

Watering can also be tricky. Yes, this plant is a succulent, but how much and how frequently you water really depends on how mature the plant is. A lot of shops sell String of Pearls plants in four-inch pots, which means that the plants are juvenile and haven't had much of a chance to establish a strong root system. For a smaller plant, water it more frequently with a smaller quantity of water. This might mean watering it twice a week, but only a few tablespoons at a time. Let that dry, then water it again. If you have a more mature plant, you can water it once every week or two with a more substantial amount of water; then let it dry out completely and water it again.

Native Habitat: *South Africa*

Calathea orbifolia

All calatheas are amazing, but the *Calathea orbifolia* is the variety that's making the most waves these days.

C. orbifolia is a gorgeous, big-leafed babe that makes a great floor plant once it has matured. Don't fret if you can only find a small plant; they are just as amazing and make a great addition to any table or shelf . . . at least until they get too big!

Like most calatheas, this variety thrives in indirect light. Too much light and you'll end up with a sunburned plant. Calatheas also need lots of water. One skipped week of watering will certainly damage your plant, so stay on top of it! If the leaves start to get brown and crisp, you're under-watering. While those leaves won't technically recover, the plant can still produce new growth, so don't be too hard on yourself. Another great thing about calatheas?

They're nontoxic for both dogs and cats.

Native Habitat: *Central and South America, Asia, and Africa*

Majesty Palm

Ravenea rivularis

Who says Victorian palms aren't making a comeback? These palms are such a vibe. An addition of a Majesty Palm to a room immediately transports the space into a tropical, lush, luxe realm. Victorians loved palms for this reason, and so do we.

The best thing about Majesty Palms is that they're so affordable. You can easily find a six-foot-tall or larger plant for under $100. If you're looking for big impact from a large plant that won't break the bank, go with a Majesty Palm. If you do purchase a smaller plant, know that Majesty Palms are slow growing.

Ravenea rivularis is nontoxic to cats and dogs.

Native Habitat: *Madagascar*

Philodendron Birkin

The variegation on the leaves of the *Philodendron* "Birkin" is exquisite, so perhaps it *is* the Birkin bag of the plant world! Basic philodendron care applies here. Give it bright, indirect light because the variegation on the leaves means that the plant will need a little more light than usual to perform photosynthesis. Bright, indirect light also helps the plant develop more defined variegation on its leaves. This philodendron will thrive in a humid environment, so get yourself a spray bottle and mist your plant multiple times a week. Water when the soil dries an inch from the surface.

Native Habitat: *Brazil*

Bird of Paradise

Strelitzia reginae

The Bird of Paradise is a plant that makes the most impact in its mature form. Yes, you can find various other sizes at your favorite houseplant source, but think twice about purchasing a smaller plant. Generally, customers purchase a Bird of Paradise for its large, lush-looking oblong leaves. In order to usher a juvenile into that large, adult form you will need patience, a ton of humidity, and . . . more patience.

Birds of Paradise plants are tropical, so they enjoy bright sunlight, well-draining soil, and lots of humidity. With the proper care, expect your plant to grow to over six feet tall with (lots of) time.

Native Habitat: *South Africa*

Aeonium

The aeonium is a gorgeous plant. The leaves grow in the shape of a flower on the end of the branches. Aeoniums are sought after for their rosette shape and the ease with which they grow, which puts them right into our windowsill category.

Aeoniums need bright, direct light. Water only when the soil dries out completely, and remember that if you have a larger plant, it will drink a larger quantity of water. Be on the lookout for signs of spider mites and aphids; aeoniums are particularly vulnerable to these pests.

Aeonium is nontoxic to cats and dogs.

Native Habitat: *East Africa and the Canary Islands*

Green Velvet Alocasia

Alocasia micholitziana "Frydek"

This one is a total stunner. The arrow-shaped leaves have thick, white veins and a soft, velvety texture. While it's absolutely gorgeous, growing it can be stressful: Alocasias need a lot of humidity to keep their leaves from browning around the edges.

This plant loves to have moist soil but hates sitting in water. Finding its "happy place" is hard work, but it will pay off. These plants thrive in a warm, humid greenhouse environment with filtered, indirect light.

Native Habitat: *Southeast Asia*

Stephania erecta

This bulbous plant has taken social media by storm. The *Stephania erecta* sprouts from its caudex, which resembles a bulb. The plant produces vertical-growing vines that are very thin and delicate with wide, deep-green leaves. The effect is almost cartoonish, which adds to the plant's appeal.

The *S. erecta* does best with indirect light and moderate watering. The plant goes dormant in the winter when the foliage dies back, which is when you should begin watering it very minimally—perhaps only once a month. Do not overwater, as the caudex will rot, and your plant will die. That being said, if you plant this in a terra-cotta pot, prepare to water more frequently.

This plant is historically at high risk for poaching, so make sure you know where your plant has been sourced from. If you can't track it down, pass.

Native Habitat: *Thailand*

YOUR LEAFY LEGACY:
Tips for Ethical Plant Buying

1. Know who you're buying from online.
The world of online plant buying and selling can get murky. You'll have to purchase the plant before the seller will send it to you, and there have been cases of social media sales where the seller simply pockets the money, doesn't send the plant (because it probably doesn't exist), and then moves the listing to another forum.

What's the scoop on your seller? Get to know them and their reputation. A quick search on two or three social media platforms should tell you what you want to know. It's rare that a scammer will try to sell on the same platform, under the same name, twice.

The seller's reputation is just as important as the health of the plant you're buying. If it feels funny to you, save yourself the hassle and find another source.

2.   Ask the seller where they source their plants from.
This applies to both online and in-person sales. If you feel like something is off, or simply have questions about where the plant was grown, ask. Ask if the plant was grown in a nursery and where that nursery is located. Most nursery-grown plants will have printed tags on them, but some retailers take them off and replace them with their own tags—so you should ask. Most nurseries and retail shops can at least give you the general vicinity where the plant was grown.

3.   Be careful when shopping for "rare" plants.
Never buy a "rare" plant from anywhere or anyone who can't tell you where it came from. If you're searching out "rare" or "difficult-to-find" plants like aroids, carnivorous plants, cacti, succulents, and epiphytes, proceed with extra caution. These are the plants that are in high demand and easily poachable from megadiverse countries.

4.   Use your eyes.
Sometimes you can spot odd inconsistencies that might signal poaching on your own. If you're at a nursery or greenhouse, look at the tray that the plants are grown in. If the plants are all similar in size, that usually means that the nurseries planted from seed or propagated around the same time. They weren't yanked from the ground and stuck in the tray.

Another red flag is if there are multiple plants of different species growing in the same pot or container. If you're poaching a plant with a shovel, it's easy to carry along the plant's neighbors when you're putting it in a container to transport. Now, this is something that can happen in large-scale nurseries, too, and is perfectly innocent. But if this is paired with something else that seems suspicious, there's a good chance the plant was poached.

How Not to Get Plant Scammed

If you're in the market and shopping online, heed these tips to keep from getting duped or caught up in an ethical conundrum. These are a few tricks that scammers use to draw you in, take your money, and then spit you out—without your dream plant.

The Angle of the Photograph

If you're involved in the houseplant world on social media, you've seen these photos. There are usually two subjects in the frame: the plant and the person holding the plant. The person is holding the plant with its leaves and crown (the center) in full view.

What you don't see is that the person is holding the plant out, straight-armed, toward the camera. This is a simple trick of perspective that makes the plant look twice (or sometimes triple) its size. A photo from this angle can make a four-inch potted plant look like an eight-inch one.

If you look in the background and objects look remarkably smaller than the plant in the foreground, you can bet the photo was taken with this trick.

Sellers will post these types of photos to trick you into thinking you're buying a much larger, fuller plant.

Pictures of the Mother Plant instead of the Plant You're Buying

When looking at a plant listing, it's very important to read the fine print. Most of the time sellers will post photos of a larger, more mature plant before posting photos of the actual plant that is for sale.

It's not unheard of for a buyer to want to know what the plant will look like when it matures, but it gets tricky when the seller isn't explicit and upfront with the customer. Be sure to read the entire listing—sometimes the information is hidden toward the bottom of the block of text and will say something like "*photo is not of the plant for sale."

Now, just because sellers post these types of photos doesn't mean they're trying to scam you. A lot of the time, the error comes with the buyer not reading the entire listing. If you don't want to be surprised when you open that plant box you got in the mail, read everything before you buy.

Price Point

Many of the gorgeous, "rare," tropical plants that everyone is pining over are selling for outrageous amounts of money. Sellers are shopping around unrooted cuttings or nodes for hundreds of dollars. A small *Philodendron* "Strawberry Shake" is currently going for upward of $600. A mature (and ever popular) *Monstera albo borsigiana* will sell for $1,000 or more.

If you stumble upon a listing of a plant that you've seen sell for a significantly higher price, the listing is probably too good to be true. You can always feel the seller out, but more than likely you'll find that it's some kind of sketchy setup that you should stay out of.

Communication and Reputation

When buying online from a seller, communication is key. Go with your gut. If you've reached out with questions about their product and you get an odd response, pass. If you find that the seller is trying to string you along, pass on that too.

Online, word travels fast. If you're curious or feeling "iffy" about a situation, ask around. If the seller has any kind of clout, folks will know. That also goes in reverse. If the seller has scammed anyone, people will usually know. Do your research.

Unrealistic Photos

Last but not least, scrutinize the listing photo. Do your research on the plant that the seller is advertising, especially if the plant has bizarre coloring or variegation. Leaves with no chlorophyll cannot survive or sustain a plant. So if you see a plant marketed with all-white leaves, it's most likely a scam or the plant has been chemically modified and will not thrive.

CHAPTER 10

Welcome to the Houseplant Family

We have journeyed through the ages of houseplants together, from the beginning of civilization to our modern world! Of all the things that have changed and evolved in our world, we can say now that the presence of houseplants has been a constant for centuries. These indoor plants have been used for things like mini-medical gardens, as the main focal point in living rooms, and as emotional-support objects.

Now, across the globe, shops and nurseries specializing in houseplants have cropped up, which makes learning about keeping plants indoors as easy as strolling down to your favorite neighborhood plant spot. Humans have the desire to keep and care for living things, and plants are no exception, but learning to keep them alive is just one part of the puzzle. It is extremely important to see the whole picture, and I hope this history of the potted plant both entertained you and, maybe, helps you become a better plant parent.

It was a very specific choice to refer to potted plants as "beasts" in the title of this book. By definition, "beast" refers to something that is difficult to control or contain. Isn't that what houseplants are? No matter what we do, or what methods we use to keep plants happy inside our homes and living spaces, they are still beasts of the wild. And that is a wonderful, beautiful thing—particularly if we make extra efforts to understand where these plants came from and how their unique journeys ended on our shelf or table or windowsill.

For Your Reference

This quick and (get your hands) dirty reference section contains all the basic info you need to know about caring for your houseplants. There is a breakdown of basic care by type: tropical, desert, and epiphytic plants; basic information on identifying common pests; water and light requirements; propagation techniques; buying tips; and container advice.

This isn't comprehensive, so don't get too excited—but it is a good place to start your plant care journey.

The Most Important Step: Selecting Your Plants

The most important step to keeping a houseplant alive is one that's often overlooked: selecting the right one! If you go into a shop or find a plant online and buy it without understanding what you're getting into for its care, or even knowing what the plant is supposed to look like, you're already in trouble.

These few, easy steps will help you secure your metaphorical sea legs when pushing off into the ocean of plant ownership.

Plan Ahead: Do Your Research

Houseplant novices should consider purchasing their plants in person before exploring the infinite online offerings available. Holding, touching, and looking at the plant in person is an entirely different experience than purchasing one online, sight unseen.

We've all seen those beautiful plant photos on social media. Plan ahead for your plant shopping trip by bookmarking a few of your favorite Insta plants to show the sales associate when you get to the store. While those particular plants might not thrive in your abode, these references will give you a jumping-off point for discussion with the plant expert to help choose the right plant for you.

Plan Ahead: Know Yourself and Your Home

Ask yourself some questions in advance: What kind of light does your living space get? How dry is the air in your home? What kind of care commitment are you willing to make? Do you travel a lot? Do you have pets? Small children? If you know the specific spot where you want your new plant to live at home, make a note of that location and any pertinent features. Is it a dark corner or near a radiator? Also keep in mind that plants don't just get taller; they also grow in diameter—so plan accordingly.

At the Shop: Ask for Help

This is a huge benefit to buying a plant in person versus online. The lovely sales associates are there to help you, so don't be afraid to ask them questions about light, watering, humidity levels, and pet toxicity. They should have plenty of advice to help you select the perfect plant for your living space so you don't rush into a purchase that you'll end up killing (or despising) within the week.

At the Shop: Inspect Your Options

Find a plant that makes you happy. Pick it up and take a good look at it. Does the foliage look healthy, or is the plant showing signs of distress? If the foliage is droopy, discolored, or crispy around the edges, try to find a different plant. Check the undersides of the leaves to make sure there are no signs of pests—no crusty residue, no white or brown specks. Take a peek down into the soil. Don't make the mistake of bringing a plant home that has a bug infestation.

At the Shop: Grab a Pot

If you're also in the market for a new pot, this is a good time to buy one. Most plant shops will repot your plant for a small fee.

While you're browsing for a new vessel, keep in mind that a clay or terra-cotta pot will wick the moisture out of the soil faster than a glazed pot. Also, terra-cotta pots have a reputation for scuffing furniture, so make sure you stick some felt pads underneath the tray before you set it on your table or other surface.

It's a good rule to size up two inches or so from the original grower's pot. Succulents and other plants with shallow root systems can be squeezed into the same size or smaller pots. Tropicals and large trees need the room to spread out.

When You Get Home: Enjoy Your Purchase

Place your plant in its new spot and enjoy it. Take a few pictures. Upload it on social media. Be a proud plant parent! Be sure to tag your plant shop!

When You Get Home: Ask Follow-up Questions

Don't be afraid to reach out to the nursery or shop where you made your purchase. If you're feeling lost or confused as a plant parent, reach out. Those businesses are happy to help you with plant care questions and concerns. There are also lots of online plant groups—on every social media platform you can think of—that offer advice and will answer all of your questions.

Remember, it's a learning experience. If you end up with a dying plant, don't be discouraged. Try again!

Tropical Plants 101

Most of the houseplants on the market are tropical plants. They're native to many of the world's rain forests and tropical regions, but common tropicals that are sold as houseplants have survived decades of selection by growers because of their ease of care and hardiness. Most of these plants have similar care instructions; however, it's always best to investigate the specific species and variety you end up with—just in case the care is more specialized.

One of the main requirements of owning a houseplant is learning how to mimic the plant's natural environment. For tropical plants, that generally means re-creating a miniature rain forest climate. It's not as hard as it sounds! But obviously one of the most important necessities is water.

Tropical plants love for their soil to stay evenly damp but not saturated. Think moist but not wet. This can sometimes be tricky to achieve, especially if you're a bit of a novice. A good way to manage your watering schedule is to observe your plant daily until you have a good understanding of how fast it dries out after being watered. Within two or three watering cycles you'll have it mastered.

Surprisingly, a lot of common tropical houseplants can tolerate being under-watered every now and then. We've all been there—you get busy and then, all of a sudden, you remember that calathea in the corner. A little trimming and patient care will bring many under-watered plants back into their prime.

However, it is rare that a plant, tropical or not, will bounce back from being *over*watered. Overwatering causes root rot, stress, and bug infestations.

It's easy to fall into the *"what if it needs a drink?"* trap. But here's the thing: Most tropical houseplants won't need a drink until the top of the soil begins to dry out. That's usually at least three days after watering, if not longer. The best way to tell is to physically touch the soil; stick your index finger a knuckle deep in the dirt and see if it's wet or damp to the touch down there. If the soil is dry to the touch on top but still damp an inch under, it's about time to get your watering can out.

Relax and take a breath. Your plant is going to tell you when it needs a drink.

Humidity

Another thing you have to consider when re-creating a tropical mini-climate is the humidity in your home. Many modern homes, with their fancy central air, are as dry as deserts inside. If your house is feeling similar, and your sinuses and skin are telling you so, you can bet that your tropical houseplants are suffering too. A few bursts of spray-bottle mist and your plants will be set, right?

Wrong.

Misting your tropical houseplants is one of the least effective things you can do to raise the humidity level in your home. Spraying the foliage with water will create a temporary bubble of humidity around your plants, but as soon as the droplets evaporate, the humidity falls back to its starting point.

However, there are a few simple things you can do that will *actually* increase the humidity around your plants—and some of them are free.

1. Group your plants together.
Grouping your tropical plants together naturally increases the humidity levels around them! Plants naturally release moisture through their leaves through a process called transpiration. One plant will release moisture, and its neighbor will soak it up.

2. Put your plants in a tray.

Get a large tray that is at least two inches deep. Fill it with pebbles or rocks. Set your plant pots with drainage holes right on top of the rocks—make sure they're balanced and won't tip over—then fill the tray with water. As that water evaporates, the plants will bask in the humidity.

3. Give plants a weekly shower.

It's never a bad idea to give your tropical plants a good soaking but note that this method should only be used if your pots have drainage holes. Once a week, collect your plants and set them in your shower. Turn the shower head to a lukewarm temperature and let your plants sit in the "rain" for five minutes. This not only increases the local humidity around your plants but also washes the leaves and takes care of your weekly watering obligations. Fiddle-leaf figs and monsteras especially love this method!

4. If you have money to spend, buy a humidifier.

Of course, if you want to shell out a few dollars, you can always buy a nice humidifier. Buy just one or put one in every room—every little bit helps your tropical houseplants make it through the dry (nontropical) winter months.

5. Light

While tropical houseplants vary in terms of light requirements (once again, do your research!), it's a safe bet that your plant will thrive in bright, indirect light.

Bright, indirect light can be described as diffused light coming from an east- or south-facing window (or near to) that is obscured with a sheer blind or frosted glass. If there's nothing fracturing the light, simply move the plant farther away from the window. Remember, bright light, not hot light. Hot light scorches their leaves.

You will find tropical houseplants that can live in lower-light conditions like dracaenas, pothos, some philodendrons, and aspidistras, but that doesn't mean those plants don't like indirect light too.

Epiphytes 101

In the world of houseplants, epiphytes are truly unique. While most common houseplants are "vascular," meaning the plant moves nutrients to all its different parts via vessels—not dissimilar to our own vascular system—epiphytes are nonvascular, with some exceptions. Some get their nutrients from, you guessed it, the air—namely the water and other stuff floating around in the air. Others get their nutrients from fungi, dust, and debris like animal droppings and decaying plant matter.

The name "epiphyte" comes from the Greek words "epi" and "phyte," meaning, "on top of plant." The word refers to the plants' growth pattern. Epiphytes grow without soil, instead attaching themselves to host plants, where they live without being parasitic. Epiphytes can be found in many tropical and temperate regions all over the globe. You can find them living in trees, in outcrops of rocks in mountainous areas, or simply on the ground among vascular plants.

Many people hear the word "epiphyte" and immediately think of tillandsias, commonly known as air plants. Yes, air plants are epiphytes, but so are lots of other common houseplants! There are plenty of orchids, ferns, bromeliads, and cacti that are also epiphytes.

Care instructions will depend on the type of epiphytic houseplant you have. While the short list below covers three of the most common epiphytic houseplants, it's always best practice to do a little bit of research on the plant you have in your home.

Common Epiphytic Houseplants

Staghorn Ferns

Mounted staghorn ferns seem to always be having a moment. They look fabulous hanging on their board mounts, no matter the design style of your home.

Staghorns have two sets of leaves that grow, one sterile and one fertile. The sterile leaf grows as a "shield," acting as protection for the shallow roots and also helping the plant attach to its host. These sterile leaves grow in green, but quickly turn brown and leathery. This is what they're supposed to look like, so leave them alone!

The fertile leaves grow from the center of the sterile leaves and are shaped like antlers, thus the name "stag horn."

Light

Staghorns, like most epiphytic plants, prefer bright, indirect light. Remember, these guys naturally grow in the canopy of the rain forests, so try to re-create that environment. Too much sun and you'll have a brown, crispy plant.

Water

Watering a mounted plant is a little different from getting that watering can out. Staghorn ferns are mounted on boards using moss and twine, and the easiest way to water them is to take the mount down and soak the whole thing. Soak it once a week, once the moss is dry.

Also, staghorns thrive in high-humidity, high-temperature environments. Don't put it in a room that drops lower than 60 degrees Fahrenheit on a regular basis.

Christmas Cacti

Christmas cacti, also known as *Schlumbergera*, are easily one of the most identifiable houseplants. This native Brazilian epiphyte has draping, green branches that produce beautiful flowers that bloom for weeks at a time. It's not really common knowledge that these plants are epiphytes in nature because many growers plant them in a dry, sandy potting mix. This works well, too, but if you have one of these in your collection, you know that their "terrestrial" root system is extremely shallow and doesn't do much to keep the plant in place. Christmas cacti do best in shallow containers, shallow hanging baskets, or mounted where they can drape. They prefer a smaller container. Repot every three or four years.

Light

Christmas cacti need bright, indirect light during the day to produce their beautiful blooms and to stay healthy. Try placing your plant in a spot that gets eastern exposure. Without proper light, these plants will grow leggy and weak. But too much light will burn your plant. In order for flower buds to form, Christmas cacti need eight hours of light and sixteen hours of darkness every day. This is why it blooms around Christmas, as the daylight hours get shorter. It is said that even turning on a light at night in the cactus's room will disrupt the cycle. Better safe than sorry—during the fall months try putting your cactus in a room that doesn't get used at night.

Water

When the plant isn't blooming, water only when the soil is dry to the touch, roughly once every seven days, depending on the light exposure and moisture level in your home. When the plant is flowering, make sure the soil is evenly damp (not soaking wet) at all times. Because of its epiphytic nature, the plant benefits from a high-humidity environment. Remember, *Schlumbergera* are not desert cacti; they are native to the rain forest and need to be treated as such. If your plant is looking wilted or shriveled, you need to keep better track of your watering habits.

Christmas cacti will not thrive in inappropriate temperatures. The ideal temperatures are 70 to 75 degrees Fahrenheit in the daytime and 60 degrees (as a minimum) at night. If your cactus is getting too cold, it will not produce blooms. Remember, this baby is from the tropics!

Phalaenopsis Orchids

As you now know if you've read through this book, orchids have been the darlings of the horticultural world for hundreds of years. Collectors spend fortunes to claim rare specimens as their own.

The phalaenopsis, also known as the moth orchid, is not rare, but it is extremely tough. These are the orchids that you see everywhere, from the florist to the discount grocery store. Billions of these guys are imported into the United States every year, and they are very affordable. For this reason, it's also the variety that's most likely to get chucked out after the blooms die back.

If cared for correctly, the moth orchid will bloom multiple times a year. They are very hardy and can take some neglect, which is why they're a perfect beginner orchid.

Do yourself a favor and avoid any plant that has been spray-painted or dyed an unnatural color. Steer clear of any neon green, blue, or yellow. If you question whether or not the orchid has been painted, run your finger gently over the petal in question. If the color comes off, you'll have your answer.

Soil

Epiphytes get almost all of their water and nutrients from the air surrounding the plant, *not the soil.*

Because of this, epiphytic orchids should never be potted in traditional potting mix. Phalaenopsis should be grown in a specialized mix made from bark, vermiculite, sphagnum moss, and perlite. It is very important for air to be able to flow between the roots of the plant. You can find premixed orchid medium in any place that sells potting mix.

If you're new to the game, it's best to pot your orchid in a container with drainage. You can find all kinds of decorative orchid pots that have holes in the sides for drainage and air circulation.

Light

As a rule, avoid direct sunlight. Phalaenopsis are extremely susceptible to sunburn. Place the orchid in a spot that gets morning or afternoon sun. A west- or north-facing window may be best, depending on your home.

If you have no choice but to put it in a window with direct sun, make sure there's a barrier between the window and the plant. A sheer blind or shade will do the trick to diffuse the light.

Water and Temperature

This is where orchid care can get a little tricky. Phalaenopsis love humidity but cannot handle being overwatered. They will also suffer if they're left to dry out. If your phalaenopsis is sitting in a cache pot (usually inside a plastic pot inside a pot with no drainage) make sure you empty the cache pot after you water your orchid. Under no circumstances should a phalaenopsis, or any epiphytic orchid, be left to sit in water.

As far as temperature goes, don't let a phalaenopsis be exposed to temperatures under 50 degrees Fahrenheit.

Common Problems

While it's difficult to diagnose every issue you might have with your epiphytic houseplant, there are a few troubleshooting tips to go over before you deep dive into Houseplant Help 101.

Does your epiphyte have a squishy, dark base? Is it soft or rotting anywhere? If so, you might have an overwatering issue that is causing your plant to rot.

Are the plant's leaves curling in on themselves? That's definitely a humidity or watering issue. Up the humidity level around your plant and water it more often.

Are you doing everything right, but maybe the plant is looking brown and crispy, even after you water it? Might be time for a trip to the plant store because there's a good chance that your plant is dead.

Arid Plants 101

Often advertised by plant shops as "drought tolerant" and "low maintenance," houseplants that come from the desert typically fall into the cacti and succulent categories. Of course, there are exceptions, but they're less common. Succulents and cacti tend to be very hardy and can withstand long periods of time without water if given the correct amount of light. Many of these plants have extremely long lifetimes and typically become lineage plants for collectors, passed down for generations.

The succulent craze ebbs and flows along with all other houseplant trends, but desert plants have literal staying power. These plants are generally compact when purchased as houseplants, so they're perfect for a small-space dweller, which adds to their popularity. Unless you're after a particularly rare variety, you'll find that desert plants are grown and sold at a relatively affordable market price.

It's true that these plants will bounce back from a fair amount of neglect, but that doesn't mean that they're immortal or indestructible. Sometimes all it takes for these plants to kick off is one solid overwatering.

Light

Desert houseplants are all about that lighting situation. If they don't get enough light, they will pale, yellow, and suffer—then begin to rot. Picture the desert in your mind. Is there much shade? Definitely not.

Cacti and succulents need lots of bright, direct light for most of the day. This is especially true if you want your plant to have a strong growth cycle each year. Minimal light will make the plant grow slowly, if at all.

Will your plant die if it's not getting prime-time light for a short period of time? Of course not. But anything longer than a month and you'll have a suffering plant on your hands.

On the flip side, remember to turn your plants every week or so to keep the flesh from getting sunburned. Sun filtering through a glass window will be much hotter, so keep an eye on parts of the plant that might sit against the glass.

Temperature and Humidity

It almost goes without saying that cacti and succulents should not be placed in a humid or moist environment. Over time, the plant will rot. The same goes for keeping one of these plants in a place that gets colder than 50 degrees Fahrenheit on a regular basis. If you move your houseplants outside in the summer, bring them in before the temperature dips in the fall. While they can take short bursts of cold air, anything longer than a few days will leave permanent damage. Any exposure to below-freezing temps that causes the plant's fluids to freeze will kill your plant.

Water

Deserts are arid, dry places that have long periods of drought. Succulents and cacti evolved over time to store water inside their bodies. A healthy plant will be firm and tight. A plant that is shriveled or wilted is in need of a good watering.

Only water when the soil is completely dried out. Most only need to be watered once every month or so, depending on the temperature and light situation. The hotter and brighter the light the plant gets, the more frequently it should be watered.

When you water your plant, water thoroughly, not just a little bit! A tablespoon of water isn't going to do the trick. Water enough that the excess comes out the bottom drainage hole of the pot. In the cooler months when the growth rate is slower, water less often.

Soil and Containers

While you can get a succulent or cactus to live in traditional houseplant potting mix, they prefer an extremely well-draining mixture that's supplemented with minerals and sand. Good news for you, many companies sell prebagged cactus soil. If you're a DIY-er, you can mix your own.

Which brings us to what type of container to use.

Even the largest cacti in the desert have surprisingly small root systems. Unlike tropical plants, desert plants often have shallow roots. This tends to get many owners in trouble, especially if they have experience with plants that will grow into the size of a specific container. Most succulents and cacti won't grow or spread at that rate. Instead, they will become overwatered and will begin to decay.

Your best bet is to plant your small to medium cacti and succulents in shallow, porous pottery or containers. This will prevent overwatering and help you out in the long run.

That being said, many people plant cacti and succulents in whatever containers they have lying around, and the plants do just fine. Fancy yogurt jars, antique cans, hanging planters, floor planters—the options are endless. If you're the type that likes to gamble with containers that have no drainage, these desert plants are the ones for you. That's a bit counter to the note above about well-draining soil, but because you're only watering your plants once every month or so, the risk for overwatering is somewhat low. If you do plant in a container without a drainage hole, try watering more frequently with a lesser amount of water.

Common Problems

While succulents and cacti are susceptible to many types of pests and issues (like all houseplants), some problems are more common than others.

Scale

Scale insects feed off the sap inside of stems and stalks of the plant. These pests rarely move once mature and look like little brown scabs.

Scale damage on succulents and cacti looks like little brown holes in the leaves and stems. Insecticidal spray won't do much for you unless you debug your plant first. Scale has a hard, protective shell, so the spray will roll right off. Use rubbing alcohol and scrub the scale off your plant, then treat with an insecticidal spray.

Cacti and succulent owners know that rot is the number one problem to watch out for. Rot can be caused by a few different issues. If you notice that the plant is rotting at the base, but you know for certain that you're not overwatering, it could be from cold exposure or soil that's holding too much moisture in the middle of the pot.

If the soil is completely saturated and you suspect you've overwatered, you might be dealing with something called basal rot disease. If you see the rot start to spread, you can cut off the rotting part of the flesh using a clean, sharp knife. If you don't catch it until it's too late, you can lop off the top of the plant above the rot and attempt to graft or propagate it.

Common Houseplant Pests

Okay, so let's talk about bugs.

As a houseplant owner, you'll come across them at some point, whether you want to or not. They can be icky, but if you know what to look for, you'll be able to identify, treat, and get rid of them in no time.

Houseplant pests tend to show up when plants are overwatered, under-watered, or exposed to other neglect. Any time a plant gets stressed, it becomes more susceptible to getting bugs. The more prepared you are, the less dramatic the entire experience will be when it happens to you.

If you notice any of these pests on your houseplants, immediately isolate the plant (and sometimes, the surrounding plants) and treat it. Keep it quarantined for at least a week after the signs of pests are gone. You can never be too careful!

Fungus Gnats

Of all houseplant pests, fungus gnats are the least damaging (unless you have a massive infestation, which is rare) but also the most annoying. They're tiny things that buzz around your plants and will eventually find their way to any ripe fruit in your kitchen.

Fungus gnats are extremely common. They have short, short life cycles of about a week, but they lay hundreds of eggs in the top centimeter of potting soil before they die off. This makes it hard to get rid of all of them because more hatch so quickly.

In order to get rid of them, let the plant's soil dry all the way out. Fungus gnats thrive on wet potting soil. Drying it out will kill the adults, the juvenile larva, and the eggs. For good measure, add a sticky trap to the pot to catch the adult gnats. If you find that simply drying the soil out doesn't work, water the plant thoroughly with what is called a peroxide flush. Dilute drugstore hydrogen peroxide—one part peroxide and four parts water—then water your plant like you always do.

Scale

While spider mites feed off the nutrients of your plants by biting and chewing foliage, scale feeds off the sap inside of stems and stalks. They rarely move and look like little brown bumps, almost like a scab.

Damage can look like leaf damage (if the foliage is turning unexpectedly brown or yellow or dying), stem damage (little brown holes), or other odd markings on your plant. This damage is almost always visible near the scale themselves, simply because they don't move much during their life spans.

If you treat scale solely with an insecticidal spray, you're not going to have much luck. Scale has a hard shell that protects its tiny body, and sprays will roll right off. Soak a Q-tip in rubbing alcohol and scrub the scale off your plant, then spray the plant.

Mealybugs

These guys are flat pests that are white and fuzzy. Much like scale, after they find a good place to chow down on your plant, they won't move around. If you spot flat, white spots on your plant, you've probably got mealybugs.

A telltale sign is what they leave behind. After they suck the sap from your plant, the mealybugs produce a sticky substance that they release on the leaves. If your plant is sticky, look for those mealys!

Grab a Q-tip and rubbing alcohol, as with scale, and wipe those pests off your plant. Then treat with an insecticidal soap.

Thrips

Thrips are kind of tricky. Unfortunately for houseplant owners, they come in all different species. Some have wings. Some don't. Some are smaller than others. It's really just a guessing game as to which kind of thrips you might end up with.

Thrips are more common on plants that have been outside. So if you just bought your plant from a fresh big-box store shipment or just got it from an online grower in a tropical region, check it for thrip damage.

Thrips are almost invisible, but you'll be able to spot them when they're feeding on a plant because they gather together in bunches. When feeding or laying eggs, they make a small hole in leaves and stems. You might find that thrip-damaged leaves turn transparent in some places.

To treat, hose the plant down with water (a shower is good for this!) and then treat with insecticidal soap.

Spider Mites

These mites are one of the most common houseplant pests and also one of the hardest to spot before a total infestation. As you may have guessed by their name, you can tell if you have spider mites by the webs they leave behind in the nooks and crannies of the leaves and stems of a plant. The mites spin fine webbing on the underside of the leaves, where they eat, breed, and hatch a population.

They lay their eggs in the cooler months, which is why it can be hard to catch them right away. Springtime is prime time for spider mites. After they hatch, they mature in under a week and then go on to lay their eggs—hundreds in just a few days. Check in all the nooks and crannies on the leaves, on the top side and the bottom. They spread very, very easily between plants.

So, what should you do if you find spider mites? Isolate and treat the plant ASAP. Start using an insecticidal soap. Spray on all sides of the foliage. You can also follow up with neem oil. If you have a major infestation, remove all the infected foliage and put it in the trash.

Potting Soil 101

Technically speaking, "potting soil" isn't soil at all, and that's one of the most important things to know about it. It's a mix of different mediums like perlite, peat, sphagnum moss, compost, vermiculite, and coco coir. The type of mix you should buy depends on the type of plants you're potting. The different mediums in the mix make sure that the potting soil is well draining and high in nutrients.

Gardening soil is not the same thing as potting soil. You'll find that gardening soil is heavy with compost and does not drain well because it was not created for container or indoor gardening. Instead, gardening soil's main purpose is to fill and supplement outdoor garden beds. Well-seasoned houseplant owners prefer a soilless mixture because regular "soil" attracts all kinds of fungi, bacteria, and other gnarly things that can harm your plants. When it comes to houseplants, stay away from it.

If your plants are less than happy or have a tendency to develop root rot, it's possible that you are using the wrong type of potting soil. Your soil might actually be sabotaging your plants' health.

So, what kind of potting soil should you use? Let's break it down.

All-Purpose

This is a cheaper generic mix that almost every brand makes. You can use it for your houseplants and for outdoor container gardening. If you're looking for a potting mix that you can use for multiple projects without worry, this is the one you want.

Organic

Organic potting soil is made from all-natural plant- and animal-based materials. Typical mediums include worm castings, compost, and other decaying plant matter. It gives an extra boost to the health of your plants. It's also a necessity if you're growing herbs or veggies and want them to remain organic throughout the growing process.

Moisture Controlling

Some plant owners choose to use a moisture-controlling potting soil. This mix has chemically modified moisture-controlling pellets, which keep the soil from drying out all the way. This allows the plant to continuously wick moisture into the roots. This seems like a good idea in theory, but it can open your plant up to issues like root rot, fungi, and fungus gnats.

Seed Starting

You'll see seed-starting potting mix hit displays in all the nurseries and big-box home improvement stores in the spring season, but you can find it year-round if you look. Seed-starting mix doesn't provide many nutrients to full-grown plants, as it's made to promote growth in seedling roots. Avoid this potting soil if you're not starting seeds.

Cactus Soil

Cactus and citrus potting "soil" is typically a mixture of regular potting mix and sand. Cacti, succulents, and citrus plants all need soil that drains extremely well, which is why the sand is key. If you're an overwaterer, you can utilize this potting mix with other plants.

Outdoor

The only real difference between this potting mix and the all-purpose mix is that it contains a high level of fertilizer, which can be very beneficial for outdoor growing. Be careful using this type of mix with sensitive tropical plants.

It's important to do a little research on the brand you're purchasing. Well-known brands stocked at big-box stores aren't always the best option for you and your plants. There's a lot of information out there, and a quick Google search will get you there.

Can you modify soil to fit your needs? Yes, in a pinch, if you start with the most basic potting soil. You can add all kinds of components to soil—like fertilizer, sand, and compost—but you can't take it away, so start slow.

Many plant owners who are unhappy with the types of potting soil available to them mix their own from scratch. While it can be more expensive because you're purchasing individual components, it usually pays for itself tenfold in your plants' health.

If you're interested in building your own soilless mix, start by mixing up a basic combination of equal parts coco coir, perlite, vermiculite, and peat. It's as easy as that! You can easily modify the recipe depending on your specific plant's needs.

Further Reading

Chapter 1: The Neolithic Era (10,000–3,000 BCE)

Looking to grow your own grains?
Try: *Small-Scale Grain Raising: An Organic Guide to Growing, Processing, and Using Nutritious Whole Grains for Home Gardeners and Local Farmers* by Gene Logsdon

Interested in learning more about indigenous North American plants?
Try: *Braiding Sweetgrass: Indigenous Wisdom, Scientific Knowledge, and the Teachings of Plants* by Robin Wall Kimmerer

Want to create the Hanging Gardens of Babylon in your home?
Try: *Wild Creations: Inspiring Projects to Create Plus Plant Care Tips & Styling Ideas for Your Own Wild Interior* by Hilton Carter

Chapter 2: Ancient Egyptians, Romans, and Greeks (3,000 BCE–350 CE)

Want to learn more about the stories behind the plants?
Try: *The Mythology of Plants: Botanical Lore from Ancient Greece and Rome* by Annette Giesecke

Interested in papyrus and its important role in creating modern civilization?
Try: *Papyrus: The Plant That Changed the World—From Ancient Egypt to Today's Water Wars* by John Gaudet

Curious about Cleopatra?

Try: *Cleopatra: A Life* by Stacy Schiff

Chapter 3: The Han Dynasty and the Introduction of Penjing (220)

Interested in learning about any of the art forms in this chapter?

Try: *Penjing: The Chinese Art of Bonsai: A Pictorial Exploration of Its History, Aesthetics, Styles, and Preservation* by Qingquan Zhao

Mountains in the Sea: The Vietnamese Miniature Landscape Art of Hòn Non Bộ by Phan Van Lit

The Little Book of Bonsai: An Easy Guide to Caring for Your Bonsai Tree by Jonas Dupuich

Chapter 4: The Middle Ages (500–1453)

Curious about the art of healing with plants during the Middle Ages?

Try: *Hildegard's Healing Plants: From Her Medieval Classic Physica* by Hildegard von Bingen

Want to know more about specific historical plants?

Try: *Fifty Plants That Changed the Course of History* by Bill Laws

Need a more detailed how-to about growing microgreens?

Try: *Microgreen Garden: Indoor Grower's Guide to Gourmet Greens* by Mark Mathew Braunstein

Chapter 5: (1492–1650)

Need to know about the Americas before Columbus?
Try: *1491: New Revelations of the Americas Before Columbus* by Charles C. Mann

Interested in learning more about the Taíno Civilization?
Try: Tainomuseum.org

Chapter 6: Early Modern France (1643–1715)

Dying to grow fruit trees in your own garden?
Try: *Fruit Trees for Every Garden: An Organic Approach to Growing Apples, Pears, Peaches, Plums, Citrus, and More* by Orin Martin

Tulips got you hooked and want to know more?
Try: *Tulipomania: The Story of the World's Most Coveted Flower & the Extraordinary Passions It Aroused* by Mike Dash

Chapter 7: The Nineteenth Century (1800–1899)

Need a refresher about the Industrial Revolution but don't have a ton of time?
Try: *The Industrial Revolution: A Very Short Introduction* by Robert C. Allen

Curious about all the ways you can plant a terrarium?
Try: *Terrariums: Gardens Under Glass: Designing, Creating, and Planting Modern Indoor Gardens* by Maria Colletti

Want to start your own greenhouse?
Try: *The Greenhouse Gardener's Manual* by Roger Marshall

Got the orchid fever?
Try: *The Orchid Thief: A True Story of Beauty and Obsession* by Susan Orlean

Chapter 8: Most of the Twentieth Century (1900–1970)

Curious about art nouveau?
Try: *Art Nouveau: The Essential Reference* by Carol Belanger Grafton

Loving the midcentury vibe in the garden?
Try: *The Midcentury Modern Landscape* by Ethne Clarke

Chapter 9: The Modern Age (1970–present)

Need a modern houseplant encyclopedia?
Try: *Plantopedia: The Definitive Guide to Houseplants* by Lauren Camilleri and Sophia Kaplan

Do you learn best with specific instructions?
Try: *The New Plant Parent: Develop Your Green Thumb and Care for Your Houseplant Family* by Darryl Cheng

Need houseplant suggestions for your home?
Try: *The Unexpected Houseplant: 220 Extraordinary Choices for Every Spot in Your Home* by Tovah Martin

Acknowledgments

While at times it seems like an author's work is solitary, a book wouldn't have legs without a team that puts full confidence and pride behind a project. I am continuously grateful for all that were involved in the process of creating this gem of a book.

Thank you to Andrews McMeel and my wonderful editor Allison Adler, who has believed in this project (and the houseplant community) from the starting line.

Taming the Potted Beast never would have been possible without the constant, positive presence of my agent, Laura Mazer. You are an absolute jewel.

The illustrations that accompany my words and the beautiful cover design are the phenomenal work of illustrator Ellie Hajdu, who seamlessly navigated my desires with a steady pen. A warm thank-you to Ellie.

Steph Susie, your photos always make me look like who I want to be. Thank you for your continuous friendship and words of wisdom.

There aren't enough ways to express my gratitude to my parents, who—for my entire life—have simultaneously held me to the ground while catapulting my dreams. I love you guys to the moon and back.

Olivia and Madeline, I promise you that one day I'll write a book about something other than plants!

A roaring thanks to the folks at the Boston Athenaeum for the amazing fellowship opportunity. The knowledge I gained added to this work tenfold— this book wouldn't be the same without all that time spent in the special collections reading room.

And Jenn, a life without you wouldn't be a life at all. Thank you for being my warm blanket, my comforting cup of tea, and my force to move forward with every project I take on.

About the Author

Molly Williams is the author of *How to Speak Flower* (Running Press, May 2023) and *Killer Plants: Growing and Caring for Flytraps, Pitcher Plants and Other Deadly Flora* (Running Press, September 2020). A born-and-raised Midwesterner, Molly lives in New England but spends much of her time visiting her family's cut-flower farm in southern Illinois. She is an avid houseplant collector, gardener, florist, and teacher of many things, including writing. If you would like to reach her, she's probably in a greenhouse somewhere, or you can visit her online at https://mollyewilliams.com and @theplantladi.

Ellie Hajdu is an illustrator and a toy designer for Folkmanis Puppets. Her work has been featured on *Saturday Night Live*, *Late Night with Seth Meyers*, and *The Late Late Show with Craig Ferguson*. She lives in the San Francisco Bay Area, and you can find more of her work at elliehajdu.com and @elliehajdu.